CW01617624

Passport to Cambridge First Certificate Rapid Revision Course

Mark Cholij

M
Macmillan Publishers
and
ela
English Language Arts

Published 1995 by Phoenix ELT
Campus 400, Spring Way
Maylands Avenue, Hemel Hempstead
Hertfordshire, HP2 7EZ

A division of Prentice Hall International (UK) Ltd

First published 1991 by MACMILLAN PUBLISHERS LTD
Reprinted 1995

Designed by Arc Design
Illustrations by Sarah Cottrill.

The publishers would like to thank the following for permission to use copyright texts: The Daily Telegraph PLC, Evening Standard Company Ltd, Express Newspapers PLC, Grafton Books, Guardian News Service Ltd, Celia Haddon, Neroli Lawson, Times Newspapers Limited, Today, Roger Voss.

The publishers would like to thank the following for permission to use copyright photographs: Bob Dear, EMA, Evening Standard Company Ltd, Fortean Picture Library, Asadour Guzelian, Chris Peterson, Solo Syndication and Literary Agency Ltd, Topham Picture Source.

The author would like to express his gratitude to the EFL staff and students at Central London College, Tottenham Court Road, London for all their help and encouragement. In particular, the author wishes to thank his own FCE students, who pre-tested the material in this book.

Printed in Malaysia

A CIP catalogue record for this book is available from the British Library

ISBN 0 333 56807 9

Contents

Introduction

This course offers an intensive revision programme designed for students preparing for the Cambridge First Certificate Examination in English. It can be used in the classroom, for homework or self-study. It is available in two editions, with and without a key to the answers.

The book has been written in response to the needs of students who, after completing an FCE course, still need to do a lot of revision before taking the exam itself.

The book offers a thorough review of the main points of grammar and items of vocabulary tested at FCE level, as well as the chance to develop writing, reading and speaking skills. The book also contains examination tips based on the author's own experience as a teacher. It is, in effect, an FCE workbook that bridges the gap between a course book and practice tests.

Each Unit:

1 has been structured in a balanced and varied way, bearing in mind the concentration span of the average student and the need for the teacher to pace each lesson effectively.

2 has the same format and is more or less the same length, enabling the teacher to calculate how much time is required to complete the book.

3 has some light relief in the form of a joke and a section of general interest on the derivation of popular idioms. The reading passages have also been carefully selected for their interest as well as their vocabulary content.

4 begins with two accuracy-building exercises that focus on the full range of grammar and vocabulary tested at FCE level. Accuracy Building 1 spotlights the devices used by examiners to distract a student from a correct answer. Accordingly, students should make sure that they know how to use all the alternatives given for each question. Accuracy Building 2 acts as an *aide memoire*, giving students an opportunity to use their selected answers in a slightly different context.

The exercises within each Unit are designed to spotlight any difficulties a student may still have in a given area. Specific headings in each unit indicate the particular areas that are being highlighted.

The most important aspect of this course – if it is to be used effectively – is the opportunity it should give the student to discuss grammar and vocabulary in context, to ask questions and to clarify doubts.

Unit 1

Accuracy building 1

Choose the most appropriate word or phrase to complete each statement. After deciding which is the correct answer, focus your attention on the alternatives. When can they be used?

1 She lives … 22 Fulham Road.
a in *b* at *c* on *d* with

2 I'll send you a postcard when I … to Rome.
a arrive *b* will arrive *c* get *d* will get

3 Our car broke … on the motorway.
a down *b* up *c* in *d* off

4 I can't … the sight of blood. It makes me feel faint.
a see *b* stand *c* support *d* bare

5 We … two weeks camping in the French Pyrenees.
a passed *b* made *c* built *d* spent

6 The church-tower clock … ten.
a hit *b* rang *c* struck *d* sang

7 …! You have passed your exam.
a Curses *b* Condolences *c* Commiserations *d* Congratulations

8 He was so angry that he began shouting at the … of his voice.
a top *b* loudest *c* highest *d* end

9 We get a lot of visitors … the tourist season.
a while *b* when *c* during *d* as

10 My car was badly … in the accident.
a damaged *b* destroyed *c* wrecked *d* harmed

11 What a lovely day! Let's go for … in the park.
a a march *b* a stroll *c* an excursion *d* a hike

12 Don't waste your spare time. Take … a hobby or a sport.
a in *b* on *c* up *d* off

13 We met on holiday at a seaside … .
a site *b* beach *c* coast *d* resort

14 Some shops display notices stating, 'We prosecute all … .'
a customers *b* shoppers *c* shoplifters *d* trolleys

15 The angry workers have decided to go on … .
a stop *b* strike *c* halt *d* standstill

16 I intend to … at a French University for a summer course.
a inscribe *b* enlist *c* subscribe *d* enrol

17 He is as cunning as a … .
a cat *b* rabbit *c* spider *d* fox

18 You'd better take an umbrella. It … it's going to rain.
a probably *b* looks as if *c* will possibly *d* is likely

19 The carpets need … .
a hoover *b* hoovered *c* hoovering *d* to hoover

20 I have not seen her … she moved to Scotland.
a for *b* during *c* since *d* until

21 We have a wide variety of vegetables. Take your … .
a choose *b* selection *c* pick *d* election

22 She is very old and hardly … goes out.
a never *b* not *c* ever *d* almost

23 We had a three-… meal for only £8.00.
a course *b* plate *c* dish *d* helping

24 The two women were wearing … hats.
a same *b* identical *c* alike *d* matching

25 Do as you are told, … you will be punished.
a unless *b* so that *c* otherwise *d* consequently

Accuracy building 2

Now complete the following statements from memory. Do not look back at the previous exercise.

1 I live … 33 Talbroke Grove.
2 I'll give you a ring when I … to London.
3 My old washing-machine is always breaking … .
4 I can't … pop music. It drives me crazy.
5 I have just … two hours cleaning your room!
6 The clock … twelve.
7 … on your exam success!
8 I opened my mouth and shouted at the … of my voice.
9 There is plenty of work … the tourist season.
10 The roof was badly … in the storm.
11 They went for a … by the lake.
12 I think I'll take … golf as a way of relaxing.
13 We are going back to the same holiday … we went to last summer.
14 … are people who steal things from shops.
15 The workers felt they had no option but to go on … .
16 I think I'll … for the First Certificate course.
17 They say he is as cunning as a … .
18 Don't hang out the washing. It … it's going to rain.
19 The carpet in the hallway needs … .
20 I have been here … 7 o'clock.
21 There's plenty of fruit. Take your … .
22 He hardly … loses his temper.
23 What are you going to have for the main … ?
24 They are … twins. I can't tell them apart.
25 Eat up your vegetables, … you will not get any ice-cream.

1

Spotlight on comparatives and superlatives

1 Complete each statement with the comparative or superlative form of the adjective or adverb in the right hand column.

1	Her suitcase was ... than mine.	heavy
2	It rained ... than usual yesterday.	heavily
3	The ... solution would be for you to go yourself.	easy
4	My cold is getting	bad
5	She is ... than she was last year.	thin
6	The Pacific is ... ocean in the world.	large
7	You are making too much noise. Can't you play ... ?	quietly
8	That was ... match I have ever watched.	exciting
9	She seems ... than usual.	depressed
10	You don't smoke. That's why you are ... than I am.	healthy

2 Finish each sentence in such a way that it means exactly the same as the sentence above it.

Tom is younger than me.
I am *older than Tom.*

1 I think Tony is better-looking than Michael.
I don't think Michael ... .

2 Anne is not as pretty as Sue.
Sue is ... .

3 It is very hot in Africa, whereas it is not so hot in England.
It is ... .

4 I know I am a bad tennis-player, but I am much better than Peter.
Peter is ... .

5 She is a slow driver, but he is even slower.
He drives ... .

6 The new machine is a lot more efficient than the old one.
The old machine works ... .

7 The first car costs £2000 and the second car costs £8000.
The second car is four ... .

8 Model A costs £1000, whereas Model B costs £6000.
Model A is not nearly ... .

9 France is three times the size of England.
France is three times ... .

10 There were not as many people as I had expected.
There were ... .

11 I don't earn as much money as you do.
I earn ... .

12 The novel he wrote is better than the film they made.
The film they made is not ... .

13 There is no difference between the two.
This one is ... .

14 If you work harder, you will earn more money.
The ... .

15 It is becoming increasingly difficult to buy a house in London.
It's getting ... .

16 I have never seen a more boring film.
That ... .

17 Alan earns £500 a week. Peter earns £300 and Paul earns £200.
Alan earns the most, and Paul ... .

18 I have three sons: Mark (14), Michael (7) and John (5).
John is my youngest son and Mark is ... .

19 Nobody in the class is as lazy as Graham is.
Graham is ... .

20 Nobody in the school plays tennis as well as Margaret does.
Margaret is ... .

Have a laugh

Two little boys were discussing their future.
'What are you going to be when you grow up?' asked one of them.
'A soldier,' answered the other.
'But what if you get killed?'
'Who would want to kill me?'
'The enemy.'
The other boy thought this over.
'OK then,' he said finally. 'When I grow up I'll be the enemy.'

Reading

Read the passages below. Following the passage, you will find five unfinished statements. Decide which of the alternatives, *a*, *b*, *c* or *d* best completes each statement.
When deciding which alternative fits best, do not rely on general impression. Look for and underline in the passage the evidence that supports each choice you make.

KILLER BLAZE

Police fear a fire, which killed one man and injured three others, was started deliberately. The blaze engulfed a three-storey building in Greyhound Lane, Streatham, on Sunday. It started around 1.20 am and quickly spread through all floors.

Firemen wearing breathing apparatus arrived around ten minutes later, and discovered a thirty-year-old man dead on the second floor. A post mortem showed he died of asphyxiation through smoke inhalation. The body is too badly burnt to be identified and police are waiting for dental records.

Firemen discovered two other people in the building who were suffering from smoke inhalation. Another man, who jumped before the Fire Brigade arrived, had a broken wrist and ankle. All were taken to St George's Hospital, Tooting and released after treatment.

Six fire engines were called to the scene, but before they could bring the fire under control, around 75 per cent of the building, which houses a second-hand shop on the ground floor, had been destroyed.

The fire spread so quickly through the building that the police now suspect it was arson. A police spokesman said, 'When no cause is known it is usual to treat any fire as suspicious. But what is noticeable about this incident is the speed of the fire taking over the building.' The spokesman added that, if the fire had been started deliberately, there was no clue as to the motive or whether the dead man was the intended victim.

Detective Superintendent Phil Whittock, in charge of the investigation, said, 'We have to be open-minded.' The police spokesman added that investigations were being held up because the building was too dangerous to enter. He said, 'It is difficult to carry on investigations in the building at the moment, and that obviously hinders our ability to discover the exact cause.'

(from the *Streatham and Tooting News*)

1 The police
a suspect the dead man of starting the fire.
b know that the fire started on the second floor.
c suspect that the fire was started on purpose.
d are only certain that the fire started around 1.20 on Sunday afternoon.

2 The police know
a the identity of the dead man.
b that shortage of oxygen caused the man's death.
c that the thirty-year-old man was burnt to death.
d that the dead man had been smoking before he died.

3 The three injured people
a had been in the building when the Fire Brigade arrived.
b were suffering from smoke inhalation.
c were not kept in hospital.
d had broken some bones when they jumped from the building.

4 The firemen
a experienced great difficulties in containing the fire.
b were unable to save any part of the building.
c prevented the fire from spreading through all the floors.
d sent for six fire engines to bring the fire under control.

5 The exact cause of the fire has not been established because
a the police have not discovered a motive.
b the police are unable to carry out a proper investigation.
c the police are being open-minded.
d the police do not know whether the dead man was the intended victim.

Spotlight on vocabulary: fire

Answer each question. Then discuss the difference between the words or phrases in italics. Give examples.

1 Does a fireman wear a *helmet* or a *bowler hat* on his head?
2 To convey water to the scene of a fire, would a fireman normally use a *bucket* or a *hose*?
3 To break down a door, would a fireman use an *axe* or a *hammer*?
4 To reach the top of a building from the outside, would a fireman use a *ladder* or a *stepladder*?
5 To put out a small fire, would you use a *bucket of coal* or a *fire extinguisher*?
6 What must every school building have, a *fire escape* or a *fireplace*?
7 What usually takes place at least once a term in a school, a *fire drill* or a *fire alarm*?
8 Is *fireproof material fire-resistant* or *inflammable*?

9 If you put a match to a piece of *combustible material*, would the material *burst into flames* or not *catch fire*?
10 If a house is burning, would you say that the house is *on fire* or *under fire*?
11 If you wish to burn a piece of paper, do you *set light to it* or do you *fire it*?
12 Does a fire *go off* or *go out*?

Spotlight on vocabulary: the police

1 If you are arrested, are you taken to a *police station* or to *police headquarters*?
2 If you are charged with an offence, are you put in a police *cell* or *cage*?
3 If you are arrested, do the police put *handkerchiefs* or *handcuffs* on you?
4 Do police cars have a *siren* or a *bell*?
5 Do the police take a *statement* or a *report* from you?
6 Does an English policeman usually carry a *gun* or a *truncheon*?
7 If a person is being chased by a policeman, is that person being *followed* or *pursued* by the policeman?
8 To investigate a matter, do the police *look into it* or *look it up*?

Spotlight on prepositions

Complete each statement with: *in*, *on* or *at*.

1 I'll see you ... a moment.
2 He is busy ... the moment.
3 You'll find the answers ... page 10.
4 I read about it ... the local newspaper.
5 Make sure you are ... time. Punctuality is important.
6 I get depressed ... times.
7 They arrived just ... time to catch the ferry.
8 They have rented a cottage ... a small island.
9 The houses of Parliament are situated ... the River Thames.
10 He is useless ... French.
11 She is fluent ... Spanish.
12 There is a small yard ... the back of our house.
13 There were three people ... the back of the car.
14 They will catch him ... the end.
15 The supermarket is ... the end of that street.

Spotlight on verbs

Complete this conversation outside a cinema with the correct form and tense of the verbs in brackets.

A I (be) sorry I (be) late. I (miss) my train. You (wait) long?
B About half-an-hour.
A Sorry!
B Never mind.
A The film already (start)?
B Yes, it (start) twenty minutes ago. You still (want) (go) in?
A No, I (not think) so. Why we (not go) for a drink instead?
B All right. By the way, you (see) Peter lately?
A No, I (not see) him for over a month. Why?
B He (owe) me £100. I (lend) him the money three weeks ago, and he (say) he (pay) me back within a week. But he (seem) (disappear)!

Spotlight on spelling

Study the words for a minute. Then read out a word to a partner. Ask him or her to spell the word aloud. Check his or her spelling.

arrested
deliberately
discussing
efficient
enjoyable
extinguish
handkerchief
identified
increasingly
inflammable
noticeable
obviously
punctuality
pursued
released
success
suffering
suspicious
wrecked
wrist

Pause for thought

Why do people say *touch wood*?

In many parts of the world people once believed that gods lived in trees, and so wood was sacred. If a person wanted help from a tree god, he reached out and touched wood. The custom continued long after people gave up that particular religious belief. Without knowing why they did it, they kept on touching or knocking on wood when they wanted to keep something bad from happening.
It is interesting to know that in some African countries people still make a special journey to a wood or a forest in order to touch the trunk of a tree for luck.

Do you touch wood for luck?

Writing

You have received an invitation to a friend's eighteenth birthday party, but it is impossible for you to accept it. Write a letter to your friend explaining this, and mentioning the present you are sending. (120 - 180 words)

Remember:
- to put your address on the right, followed by the date underneath. This is an informal letter, so do not put the address of the person you are writing to.
- to divide your letter into 3 or 4 paragraphs.
- to begin each new sentence with a capital letter.
- to sign off informally. Do not use *Yours sincerely* or *Yours faithfully.*

Avoid:
- sentences that are long and complicated.
- constructions that you are unsure of.
- words that you cannot spell!

Some useful phrases:
Thank you for inviting me to ...
I wish I could ..., but ...
Unfortunately, I shall not be able to ...
Although I cannot ..., I would like to send you ...
I hope you have a marvellous day and a really good time at the party.
I shall be thinking of you ...
I am truly sorry that I shall not ...
Best wishes/All my love ...

1

Speaking

1 Describe the scene. What has happened? Does the girl appear to be in pain? What is the man holding? What does he intend to do?
2 What is the best way of treating a minor burn?
3 What are the most frequent causes of fire in the home?
4 Accidents in the home are fairly common. What is the most serious accident that you have ever had?
5 What precautions should you take to avoid accidental fires and accidents in the home?

Unit 2

Accuracy building 1

Choose the most appropriate word or phrase to complete each statement. After deciding which is the correct answer, focus your attention on the alternatives. When can they be used?

1 The office is ... the second floor.
a in *b* at *c* into *d* on

2 You ... better ring him straightaway.
a should *b* would *c* had *d* must

3 It's been ... with rain since early morning.
a falling *b* pouring *c* dripping *d* dropping

4 She decided to break ... her engagement to the oil millionaire.
a off *b* up *c* out *d* in

5 If I were you, I ... accept the job.
a will *b* would *c* certainly *d* won't

6 My teacher calls me ... my first name, but I address him more formally.
a with *b* from *c* by *d* at

7 I am sure they are twins. They are so ... .
a like *b* likely *c* likeness *d* alike

8 He used ... a professional footballer.
a be *b* to be *c* to being *d* for being

9 She didn't misbehave at all. She was as good as ... .
a dead *b* gold *c* new *d* lost

10 I went to the airport to see my daughter ... .
a good-bye *b* through *c* off *d* home

11 He applied the ... too quickly and skidded off the road.
a brakes *b* tyre pressure *c* steering wheel *d* horn

12 The ship sank ... the coast of Scotland.
a nearby *b* off *c* against *d* next

13 She ... as she read the letter, and I realised that something was the matter.
a smiled *b* nodded *c* grinned *d* frowned

14 You smell awful! It's about time you ... a bath.
a have *b* will have *c* had *d* to have

15 '... of the dog!'
a Attention *b* Beware *c* Watch out *d* Look out

16 I need to go to the post office. I am ... stamps.
a needing *b* lacking *c* out of *d* missing

17 I wish I ... speak French fluently.
a would *b* could *c* can *d* should

18 I have ... friends now than when I was younger.
a less *b* least *c* fewer *d* most

19 The Cheetah is the … running animal on earth.
a faster *b* more rapid *c* quickly *d* fastest

20 Danger! Do not … out of the window or open the door when the train is moving.
a look *b* jump *c* lean *d* peer

21 One of the oldest wedding customs still observed today is the wearing of the bridal … .
a mask *b* veil *c* disguise *d* hood

22 Do you … a drink this evening?
a like *b* fond *c* fancy *d* wish

23 … jacket is this?
a Of whom *b* Who *c* Whose *d* Who's

24 Lack of funds prevented him … with his studies.
a to continue *b* with continuing *c* continue *d* from continuing

25 He … his brains trying to find a solution to the problem.
a tortured *b* blew out *c* scratched *d* racked

Accuracy building 2

Now complete the following statements from memory. Do not look back at the previous exercise.

1 Our flat is … the fifth floor.
2 You … better do it as soon as possible.
3 It's … with rain.
4 Unfortunately my girlfriend broke … the engagement.
5 If I were you, I … see a lawyer.
6 She calls her stepfather … his first name.
7 They all look … to me. I can't see any difference.
8 We used … close friends when we were at school.
9 He behaved perfectly. He was as good as … .
10 I went with Mary to the station to see her … .
11 The … failed and he crashed into a tree.
12 The island you seek is … the coast of Norway.
13 He … when he saw how large the electricity bill was. He was certainly not amused.
14 It's about time you … a haircut.
15 '… of the bull!'
16 I've been running. That's why I'm … breath.
17 I wish I … fly like a bird.
18 He is definitely improving. He is making … mistakes than before.
19 He is the … sprinter in England.
20 It is dangerous to … out of a train window.
21 She is wearing a … over her face.
22 What do you … for dinner tonight?
23 … book is that? Is it yours?
24 A violent storm prevented us … on our journey.
25 He … his brains all night, but he could not think of a way out of the dilemma he was in.

2

Spotlight on the passive

Finish each sentence in such a way that it means exactly the same as the sentence above it.

They grow coffee in Brazil. Coffee is *grown in Brazil.*

1 All the staff respect Mr Brown.
Mr Brown … .

2 We treat our customers with respect.
Our … .

3 Chemicals are polluting the air.
The air … .

4 They will hold the meeting this afternoon in Room 5.
The meeting … .

5 You should leave the meat in the oven for one hour.
The meat … .

6 They found the missing documents in his coat pocket.
The missing … .

7 Somebody saw you near the scene of the crime.
You … .

8 They were unloading the ship when they discovered the fire.
The ship … .

9 Nobody has spoken to me like that before!
I … .

10 They have built a new bridge over the river.
A new bridge … .

11 I dislike people telling me what to do.
I don't like … .

12 You should have done the work yesterday.
The work … .

13 Somebody must have repaired it last week.
It … .

14 They know he is a thief.
He … .

15 They believe he is hiding somewhere in Peru.
It … .

16 People say that he kept all his money hidden under a mattress.
He … .

17 The vacuum-cleaner needs to be repaired.
The vacuum-cleaner needs … .

18 I shall get someone to mend it tomorrow.
I shall have … .

19 Has somebody cut your hair?
Have you … ?

20 They made him work an extra shift.
He was … .

2

Reading

Read the passage below. Following the passage, you will find five unfinished statements. Decide which of the alternatives, *a*, *b*, *c* or *d*, best completes each statement.

TICKETS PLEASE

A few days ago, on the 17.16 train from King's Cross to Peterborough, I was arrested by a man in uniform. I was not drunk or disorderly. I was not smoking in a non-smoking compartment. I was sitting quietly in a standard class compartment holding a standard class 'Supersaver' return ticket, about to read my newspaper, when I was arrested. I mean, literally, arrested.

At 16.45 that day, I had gone to King's Cross station and asked for a Supersaver return ticket to Peterborough. 'Which train are you catching?' asked the clerk. 'The 17.16,' I told him as I passed my Access card under the glass. 'When are you returning?' he asked. 'Tomorrow, Thursday, in the morning,' I replied. 'That will be £17.50,' he said taking the card, processing the transaction and passing me the two part ticket, one marked Out and the other Return.

Some ten minutes out of King's Cross, two inspectors entered the carriage and one of them asked to see my ticket. Apparently satisfied, he returned the ticket to me and moved on. A few minutes later, he returned and asked to see my ticket once more. He then pronounced my ticket invalid. It was the outward portion of a Supersaver ticket and it was not valid on the 17.16 train.

I told him that I had bought the ticket less than an hour earlier and had stated which train I intended to use and that the decision as to how much to charge had been that of the ticket clerk. This was, he said, not his concern. The ticket was invalid and I would have to pay the full fare. This I declined to do. I also refused to give my name and address when asked to do so.

'I have three alternatives,' he said. 'The first is to obtain from you the full fare. The second is to obtain your name and address. The third is to arrest you.' This struck me as being rather excessive and very slightly amusing. The idea of an inspector arresting a passenger! But he was serious. He stood by my shoulder and informed me that he was now formally putting me under arrest. He moved away while I considered my position. I have never been arrested before. I did not feel very different.

The train stopped at an intermediate station and he approached me again. He asked me if I would now leave the train with him and accompany him to find a police officer so that I could be detained. Again this struck me as being rather excessive, so I declined. Would I be dragged off the train struggling and screaming? I thought I should wait and see.

The minutes went by and I thought of my wife waiting for me in the car outside Peterborough station. And I thought of the other passengers. The other passengers were another factor altogether and I am quite sure my uniformed fellow citizen knew what was going on in their minds. I looked around and saw not the merest trace of solidarity. One was looking decidedly ugly and was beginning to mutter insults.

All I had to do was give him my name and address. I capitulated and passed him my business card. That wouldn't do. I could have got it off anyone. I showed him twenty identical business cards and told him it was all right. I was who the cards said I was and I could be contacted at the address shown.

He then stood at my shoulder and 'unarrested' me. I mean that. He uttered a form of words, like a magic spell, that released me into the free world again. Phew!

(adapted from an article in *The Guardian*)

1 The author of this article was arrested
a for refusing to give his name and address to the police inspector.
b because his ticket was not valid.
c because he had refused to leave the train.
d because he had left the inspector with no other option.

2 The author
a had paid £17.50 in cash for the ticket.
b had bought the ticket on Wednesday at about 4.45 pm.
c had purchased his ticket at about 5.15 pm.
d had bought two tickets: a single and a return.

3 The author
a should have known that he was on the wrong train.
b had wanted a cheap day return ticket to Peterborough.
c had had no reason to suppose that his ticket might be invalid.
d had deliberately misled the ticket clerk.

4 The other passengers
a had given the author no support whatsoever.
b had sympathised with the author.
c had expressed their solidarity by insulting the inspector.
d had all been in an ugly mood.

5 Having finally given in, the author
a paid the full fare.
b resolved the matter by producing his business card.
c then found that it was not so easy to prove his identity.
d wrote down his name and address as proof of his identity.

Spotlight on irregular verbs

Give the past simple and past participle of each of the following verbs.

eat
eat ate eaten

become	catch	fall
begin	choose	feed
bend	come	feel
bite	cost	find
blow	cut	fight
break	dig	fly
bring	do	forget
build	draw	freeze
burn	dream	get
buy	drive	give

Spotlight on vocabulary: travelling by train

Answer each question. Then discuss the difference between the words or phrases in italics. Give examples.

1 To find out when a train is due to arrive or depart, would you consult a *railway timetable* or a *rail network*?
2 If luggage is left on a train, is it taken to the *left-luggage office* or the *lost property office*?

3 Inside a compartment, would you place your suitcase *in a luggage van* or *on a luggage rack*?
4 Does a commuter train carry *freight* or *passengers*?
5 If you wanted to buy something to eat or drink on a train, would you make your way to the *buffet car* or the *fast food restaurant*?
6 At the point where a road crosses a railway line, would you normally find a *level crossing* or a *pedestrian crossing*?
7 Is a section of railway line called a *route* or a *track*?
8 Is an express train pulled by a *tractor* or a *locomotive*?
9 Do you find *signals* or *signposts* along a railway track?
10 Does a ticket inspector usually *stamp* or *punch* your ticket?
11 Do you *set out on* or *set off* a journey?
12 Do you *make* or *do* a journey?
13 Do you *climb* or *board* a train?
14 If you need to take another train, do you *change* or *exchange* trains?
15 In a station, are general announcements made by a *spokesman* or over a *loudspeaker*?

Have a laugh

The Irish astronaut was telling his friend about Ireland's space programme.
'We're not bothering at all with the moon,' he said. 'We're flying to the sun.'
'The sun!' exclaimed his friend. 'But if you get within fifty thousand miles of it, your spaceship will just melt away.'
'We've thought of that,' said the astronaut. 'We're going at night.'

Spotlight on prepositions

Complete each statement with *in*, *on*, *of* or *off*.

1 It is ... the other side ... the street.
2 He has rented a cottage ... the mountains.
3 We are going there ... July.
4 We are moving house ... July 5.
5 I'd like to congratulate you ... your exam results.
6 I am proud ... you!
7 He takes great pride ... his appearance.
8 She prides herself ... her command ... the English language.
9 They cured him ... the disease.
10 He died ... a heart-attack.
11 She is ... her food.
12 He succeeded ... convincing her ... his honesty.
13 There is no truth ... that rumour.
14 He went off ... that direction.
15 He fell ... his bicycle.

Exam tip

➪ Do not rely on luck for the exam! Systematic revision is the key to exam success. The first step is to plan a realistic revision timetable that you will follow from now until a few days before the exam.

➪ Vary your daily revision programme as much as possible and allow yourself time for a number of short breaks while studying. Learning by heart is only effective if you concentrate on quality not quantity. Do not try to learn long lists of words all at once. Learn a few items at a time and learn them well.

Spotlight on verbs

Complete the conversation below with the correct form and tense of the verbs in brackets.

A You (type out) the report yet?
B Yes, here you (be).
A Thanks.
B Er, it (be) all right if I (go) home early today? My car (need) (service) and my local garage (shut) at five.
A This (be) the third time this week that you (ask) for time off work. On Monday you (say) that your cat (be) ill and that you (have) (take) it to the vet before five o'clock. On Tuesday you (ask) me if you (be able) (go) home early because you (not feel) well, and now today you (ask) me (let) you (leave) early! What (be) more, you only (start) this job last week! It (be) really necessary (have) your car (service) today? It (not be able) (do) at the weekend?
B I (go) away this weekend. I (not suppose) I (be able) (leave) work early on Friday afternoon, I (be able)?

2

Spotlight on spelling

Study the words for a minute. Then read out a word to a partner. Ask him or her to spell the word aloud. Check his or her spelling.

accompany	freight
address	luggage
apparently	programme
beginning	pedestrian
business	restaurant
carriage	straightaway
commuter	struggling
daughter	unfortunately
definitely	Wednesday
excessive	sympathised

Writing

You are the Principal of the Elizabeth School of English. Make a speech welcoming a group of new students to your school. (120 – 180 words)

Remember:

- to give your speech a coherent structure. Begin with a very clear introduction, saying who you are and why you are giving the speech. Make the main part of your speech flow naturally from one point to the next. Finish your speech in a logical and natural manner.
- that you are speaking to a group of people, not writing a school prospectus. Make appropriate comments as you inform them of what your school has to offer.
- to always give yourself sufficient time to thoroughly check what you have written.

Some useful phrases:
Welcome to …
First of all, let me introduce myself.
I shall not keep you long.
I'd like to say a few words about …
I am sure you would like to know …
There are some school rules which …
We ask our students not to …
You will see from your individual timetables that …
You will find the school library on …
We have a school canteen where …
Social activities include …
If you are worried about …
Should you have any problems, please do not hesitate to …
I am usually free from … to …

Pause for thought

Why do people say *fingers crossed*?

Long ago, when two people wanted the same thing to happen, one of them would hold out an index finger (the finger next to the thumb) and the other would lay his index finger against it,making a cross. The cross was a symbol which they thought would bring good luck, and among Christians it also stood for unity.

Over the years the belief in crossed fingers gradually changed. It was thought that one person alone could magically make a wish come true if he crossed his middle finger over his index finger. Finally, it was just enough to say, 'I'll keep my fingers crossed,' which simply means,' I wish that nothing may happen to spoil my chances.'

Does this expression exist in your own language?

Spotlight on pronunciation

Read out the following sentences, making sure that you pronounce each word correctly.

1 Rough is the opposite of smooth.
2 That meat is as tough as leather.
3 I've got a bad cough.
4 They made a thorough search of the area.
5 He looked through the keyhole.
6 It looks as though you were right after all.
7 Farmers plough their fields.
8 Have you visited Edinburgh castle?
9 You are not listening to what I am saying.
10 I wish you would stop whistling.
11 The doctor said my daughter had a sore throat.
12 Bill feels ill.
13 He filled his flask with water and then crossed the fields.
14 We spent a fortnight on the Isle of Man, which is an island off the coast of England.
15 I now know that the new fish and chip shop doesn't sell chocolate.
16 They spent the whole day digging holes in the garden.
17 Did you manage to find a garage?
18 I'd like to sit in the front row.
19 They had a row two days ago and are still not on speaking terms.
20 Why is she in tears? Did she tear her new frock?
21 Lead is a very heavy metal.
22 Dogs must be kept on a lead.
23 You reap what you sow.
24 I'd better sew on a couple of buttons.
25 Who is going to iron those shirts?
26 He is in debt.
27 He is a mountain climber.
28 There is no doubt whatsoever.
29 My husband is a plumber.
30 Nobody could answer the question.

2

Speaking

1 Describe the scene in the photograph.
2 Explain what you think has just happened.
3 What is the most dangerous form of transport in your country and why?
4 What is your favourite form of transport and why?
5 If you were going round the world, how would you travel and why?

Unit 3

Accuracy building 1

Choose the most appropriate word or phrase to complete each statement. After deciding which is the correct answer, focus your attention on the alternatives. When can they be used?

1 Are you interested … politics?
a about *b* in *c* of *d* by

2 If you … a ghost, how would you react?
a see *b* would see *c* will see *d* saw

3 What experience have you … of this type of work?
a made *b* had *c* done *d* managed

4 I … from rheumatism.
a hurt *b* pain *c* suffer *d* endure

5 He works … a barman in his spare time.
a like *b* for *c* behind *d* as

6 You can tell the dog is happy because it is … its tail.
a shaking *b* flapping *c* stirring *d* wagging

7 Despite all their efforts, they were … to trace her.
a unable *b* unwilling *c* incapable *d* disabled

8 We still need to buy … furniture for the living-room.
a a piece *b* some *c* much *d* one

9 He shook his … at me and threatened to hit me.
a hand *b* wrist *c* thumb *d* fist

10 How well do you … on with her?
a get *b* keep *c* go *d* carry

11 She is very … of her two nieces.
a kind *b* attached *c* affectionate *d* fond

12 Could you check the roof? I think some of the … are loose.
a bricks *b* layers *c* tiles *d* foundations

13 I'll lend you the money … I get it back before the end of the month.
a unless *b* provided *c* as long *d* condition that

14 To cheer her up , he bought her a … of flowers.
a collection *b* set *c* bundle *d* bunch

15 He is away on a business … to New York.
a trip *b* journey *c* travel *d* voyage

16 If you do not know the meaning of a word, look it … in a dictionary.
a for *b* up *c* about *d* through

17 She has got a nasty cough and a … throat.
a sour *b* sick *c* sore *d* suffocating

18 She is as busy as … .
a an ant *b* a horse *c* a bee *d* a squirrel

19 The camel is known as the 'ship of the … '.
a oasis *b* desert *c* sand *d* dessert

20 When somebody is really … , we say that he or she is as stubborn as a mule.
a conceited *b* ill-tempered *c* arrogant *d* obstinate

21 Could you … off the meeting until tomorrow?
a call *b* put *c* ring *d* set

22 He went on to become a teacher after … from university.
a graduating *b* passing out *c* leaving *d* abandoning

23 She promised she … do it, but she didn't.
a will *b* was going *c* would *d* definitely

24 There were … grazing on the hillside.
a sheep *b* a flock of sheep *c* shepherds *d* lamb

25 I am … up with your behaviour.
a put *b* tired *c* fed *d* sick

Accuracy building 2

Now complete the following statements from memory. Do not look back at the previous exercise.

1 I am not interested … such things.
2 What would you do if you … someone drowning?
3 I have … some experience of working with children.
4 I … from backache.
5 She works … a part-time cleaner.
6 The dog jumped up and down, … its tail.
7 I'm afraid I'm … to help you.
8 We bought … furniture yesterday.
9 He hit me with his … and broke my jaw.
10 They … on well with each other.
11 Most children are … of sweets.
12 He bought some … to cover the bathroom walls.
13 You can borrow my car … you drive very carefully.
14 How much did you pay for that … of grapes?
15 The school is organizing a … to the seaside.
16 I don't know his telephone number. I'll have to look it … in the directory.
17 What do you recommend for a … throat?
18 'As busy as a … ' is an example of a simile.
19 They crossed the Sahara … in a jeep.
20 He can be very … , you know. I don't think he'll change his mind.
21 Don't … off till tomorrow what you can do today.
22 After … from university, Thomas joined the army.
23 He promised he … come as soon as possible.
24 The … were scattered all over the hillside.
25 He is … up with everything at the moment.

Spotlight on reported speech

Finish each sentence in such a way that it means exactly the same as the sentence above it.

'Be quiet, Tommy!' She told *Tommy to be quiet.*

1 'I am going to Spain next week.'
She said … .

2 'I'll see you tomorrow, Paul.'
She told … .

3 'Don't wait up for me as I shall be home very late,' she said to her mother.
She told … .

4 'We have never been to Italy, but we hope to go there one day.'
He said … .

5 'I may see you tonight, Julie.'
He told … .

6 'It's raining and someone has taken my umbrella.'
He complained that … .

7 'Would you like to spend next weekend with us on our yacht?'
They invited us … .

8 'Don't forget to ring me next Tuesday.'
She reminded me … .

9 'Please do not smoke in here.'
She asked us … .

10 'I forgot to order some spare parts.'
He admitted that … .

11 'I gave it to you last week.'
He reminded her that … .

12 'I must finish the report as soon as possible.'
He said … .

13 'If I were you, I'd sell the car.'
He advised me … .

14 'How about going to Wales this weekend?'
She suggested … .

15 'Why don't you give Mary a ring?' he suggested to me.
He suggested … .

16 'What do you do for a living, John?'
She asked … .

17 'Is everything all right?'
She asked … .

18 'Do you live in a flat?'
He asked me … .

19 'Why did you steal the money, Henry?'
He asked Henry … .

20 'How much are the red apples?'
I asked the shopkeeper … .

3

Spotlight on irregular verbs

Give the past simple and past participle of each of the following verbs.

speak *spoke* *spoken*

hear
hide
hurt
keep
know
lay
lie
mean
ride
ring
shake
shine
shoot
sing
sleep
slide
steal
stand
tear
win

Have a laugh

A young lady went to a fortune-teller to have her fortune told.
'I will answer two questions for £100,' the fortune-teller said.
Although she was surprised at the amount she had to pay, the young lady gave her the money. 'Don't you think that £100 is rather a lot of money for just two questions?'
'Yes, it is,' answered the fortune-teller. 'Now, what is your second question?'

Reading

Read the passage below. Following the passage, you will find five unfinished statements. Decide which of the alternatives, *a*, *b*, *c* or *d*, best completes each statement.

WEALTHY AND WISE

It took twenty years for Stephan Sander to build up his fortune, and just a few weeks to give it away. A property tycoon who was worth £50 million, he is giving away £49 million to the Third World.

'You can only drive one car at once,' he said yesterday. 'You can only eat so much food. All of the money after that is just an ego trip. I'd make a million one year and another the next, and it did not make any difference to my lifestyle. Making the money was like going on a hunt. You'd have the chase, then the kill, then you'd start all over again. I decided enough was enough.'

Mr Sander began life in poverty in Pakistan and India, before arriving in England as a refugee. He moved to Canada in 1970, giving up teaching to make his fortune in property. Now he hopes his generosity will spur more of the super-rich to follow suit. He said: 'I want to make them feel uncomfortable about having so much. Poverty kills one hundred and fifty million people every year. That's three times the population of Britain.

A Sikh, he is fond of quoting religious passages. He said: 'As the Scripture says,what profit has a man if he acquires the whole world and loses his own soul?'

Even when the money was rolling in, Mr Sander never lived a life of extreme luxury. His three-bedroomed house has no swimming pool or tennis court. The family has two cars, the newest four years old. His eight children were never spoilt. 'I never threw money at them,' he said. 'I simply said they should take enough for their needs but any in excess they were not going to have.'

His wife Nancy, also a property expert, fully supported his decision to give away the bulk of their fortune. The couple say they still have more than enough for a happy lifestyle. 'What have we given away?' she said. 'We are not suffering. We are not advocating that people shouldn't live well or wear good clothes. The children will have less than they might, but they'll still have a good start in life.'

The Sanders' property empire has now been turned over to a charity foundation, the Consciousness International Foundation. But one thing Mr Sander is keeping is his hardened business sense. He has a reputation for being tough to deal with and has no intention of indiscriminately hurling his fortune at the Third World. 'It's easier to make money than give it away,'he said.

(from an article in *Today*)

1 Mr Sander
a is a former teacher.
b had wealthy parents.
c made his fortune in England.
d left his own country because he wanted to make a lot of money.

2 It is quite clear from the passage that Mr Sander
a was once fond of hunting.
b has been influenced by his religion.
c cares more about the Third World than his own family.
d regards money as evil.

3 By giving away his money, Mr Sander
a hopes to save one hundred and fifty million people every year.
b will be reduced to poverty.
c hopes to prevent his children from becoming spoilt.
d hopes to encourage others to do the same.

4 Nancy Sander
a thinks that people shouldn't live well or wear good clothes.
b wants her children to know what it is like to be poor.
c approves of her husband's attitude to wealth.
d believes that money is not necessary for a happy lifestyle.

5 It is evident from the passage that Mr Sander
a was in sole control of his property empire.
b is too kind-hearted to be a businessman.
c intends to set up a charity foundation.
d plans to distribute his money in a business-like way.

Spotlight on vocabulary: money

Answer each question. Then discuss the difference between the words or phrases in italics. Give examples.

1 Do parents give their children *petty cash* or *pocket-money*?
2 Is small change usually carried in a *purse* or a *wallet*?
3 Do you have to pay *income tax* or *poll tax* on the money you earn?
4 If you are prudent with your money, does that mean you spend your money *wisely* or *extravagantly*?
5 If your bank account is in the red, are you in *credit* or *overdrawn*?
6 If you find it difficult to make ends meet, are you *hard-up* or *well-off*?
7 If you are mean, are you *reluctant* or *willing* to part with your money?
8 If you have no money, are you *stingy* or *broke*?
9 If you are living in poverty, are you *poorly* or *as poor as a church mouse*?

10 Which can you spend, a *bank's notepaper* or a *banknote*?
11 If you have a mortgage, have you *lent* or *borrowed* money to buy a house?
12 Do you *settle* or *pay for* a bill?
13 Do you *exchange* or *cash* a cheque?
14 Do you *make out* or *draw out* a cheque?
15 If you receive money to help finance your studies, do you receive a *grant* or an *allowance*?
16 If your employer decides to increase your salary, do you get a *pay rise* or a *pay raise*?
17 Does a firm go *penniless* or *bankrupt*?
18 Do you *pay off* or *pay up* a debt?
19 If something is very valuable, is it *very good value for money* or is it *worth a great deal of money*?
20 In some jobs, you are able to get back the money you spend on travelling, hotel accommodation etc. Does this mean that your *expenses are paid* or that your *money is refunded*?

Spotlight on prepositions

Complete each statement with *in, on, to* or *at*.

1 I'm not disappointed. … the contrary, I'm very pleased.
2 All our efforts were … vain.
3 He is very keen … swimming.
4 Did you have anything particular … mind?
5 The prisoner was forced to live … bread and water for a week.
6 He crept into the room … tiptoe.
7 He discovered … his horror that he had left his passport behind.
8 She watched … horror as the little boy ran across the busy road.
9 She looked … him … disgust.
10 She listened … the news … amazement.
11 … my great surprise, he invited me … his party.
12 I met her … a party.
13 It is rude to stare … people.
14 Please do not point your finger … me!
15 No one can predict what will happen … the future.

Pause for thought

Why do many people think it is bad luck to spill salt?

This belief goes back to the days when salt was so precious that any loss of it might truly cause hardship.

The words *salt* and *salary* are said to be closely related, since *salary* comes from the Latin word *salarium meaning salt money.* Salt used to be a means of payment many years ago, and in many countries it was rare, and therefore a prized food ingredient. Amongst other things, it was used to preserve meat.

It is also said by others that the word *salt* is derived from *Sallus*, the daughter of the Roman God of health. Whichever is true, salt was valued and important substance.

If you do spill salt, you can avoid bad luck by throwing a little of the spilt salt over your left shoulder!

3

Spotlight on verbs

Complete the conversation below with the correct form and tense of the verbs in brackets.

A You (hear) the news?
B News? What news?
A Andrew (promote) to assistant manager.
B You (joke)! When all this (happen)?
A Just this morning. The managing director (come) into our office at about 9.30 and (ask) (see) him. Twenty minutes later Andrew (come) back with a huge grin on his face.
B It (make) you sick, it (not do)! How long Andrew (be) with this company? Six months?
A A bit longer. He (arrive) about the same time as Anne (do).
B Well, I (be) with this company since I (leave) school, over five years ago.
A Yes, but you (not be) married to the managing director's daughter!

Spotlight on spelling

Study the words for a minute. Then read out a word to a partner. Ask him or her to spell the word aloud. Check his or her spelling.

accommodation	consciousness	mortgage	reputation
acquire	cough	niece	scattered
affectionate	desert	recommend	squirrel
behaviour	dessert	religious	stirring
conceited	loose	reluctant	stubborn

Exam tip

In Paper 2 you will have to write two compositions in one and a half hours. Devote equal time to both compositions.

For each composition:
- allocate ten minutes for planning and making concise notes.
- spend twenty-five minutes writing the composition.
- give yourself ten minutes to check and re-check what you have written. If in doubt, cross it out!

Writing

You have just started your first job. Write a letter to a friend, describing the job and saying how you feel after your first few days at work. (120 – 180 words)

Some useful phrases:
Great news! I have finally got a job!
I have managed to find a job at last!
You won't believe this, but ...
I started my first job last ...
I am working as/in a ...
My work involves ...
I spend most of the day ...
I get on well with most of the staff, but there is one person who ...
I am not used to working under such pressure.
I am sure I shall soon get used to ...
What I dislike most about the job is ...
I am sure that if I work hard ...
I'll let you know how I get on.

3

Speaking

1 Imagine that you are describing this photograph to somebody who has not seen it. What would you say?
2 Do you feel giddy just looking at the photograph? Do you have a head for heights? Which jobs or leisure activities require a head for heights?
3 Do you think that the man's job is particularly dangerous? Do you think that he deserves to earn a lot of money for working at such a great height?
4 Is there any particular job that you would not do, even if you were paid a great deal of money, because you consider it far too dangerous?
5 When choosing a job, which is more important in your opinion: job satisfaction or the amount of money you will earn?

Unit 4

Accuracy building 1

Choose the most appropriate word or phrase to complete each statement. After deciding which is the correct answer, focus your attention on the alternatives. When can they be used?

1 Many people are ... of spiders.
a amused *b* allergic *c* attacked *d* afraid

2 Is she a friend of ... ?
a yours *b* you *c* your *d* you're

3 The ... of ships entered the harbour.
a herd *b* shoal *c* fleet *d* pack

4 You ought to be in bed. It's ... past midnight.
a considerable *b* largely *c* well *d* very

5 Cats have very sharp ... .
a paws *b* claws *c* jaws *d* nails

6 My grandmother is still very active ... her age.
a despite *b* although *c* in spite *d* though

7 There is growing recognition that smokers ... the health and lives of non-smokers.
a danger *b* endanger *c* dangerous *d* dangerously

8 Our cat was ... over by a bus yesterday.
a knocked *b* hit *c* trodden *d* run

9 Dogs are known to have a highly developed ... of smell.
a ability *b* talent *c* sensitivity *d* sense

10 The world's first underground railway was the Metropolitan Railway, which was opened in London in 1863. That is ... .
a a fact *b* a quote *c* a suggestion *d* an opinion

11 He has promised to change his ways. He is going to turn over a new ... .
a page *b* chapter *c* leaf *d* beginning

12 I wouldn't rely on him. He is always letting people ... .
a off *b* down *c* out *d* go

13 She got off her bicycle and walked up the ... hill.
a steep *b* sloping *c* crooked *d* bent

14 Golf is played on a golf ... .
a pitch *b* course *c* court *d* track

15 One of the greatest ... in medical science was that of Penicillin by Alexander Fleming in 1928.
a invention *b* inventions *c* discovery *d* discoveries

16 Every six months I see my dentist for ... .
a an overhaul *b* a check-up *c* checking out *d* an exam

17 Stonehenge is a prehistoric monument, ... from about 1500 BC.
a dating *b* aged *c* origin *d* going back

18 Black cats are … to be unlucky.
a told *b* mentioned *c* believed *d* say

19 All her friends were envious when she came back from holiday with a lovely sun … .
a tan *b* stroke *c* bronze *d* burn

20 Mr Jones … pigs for a living.
a brings up *b* gives birth to *c* breeds *d* cultivates

21 I wonder why she has not written. I haven't heard … her for a very long time.
a of *b* from *c* about *d* news

22 If you have a question, please … your hand.
a lift *b* rise *c* raise *d* set up

23 Would you mind … in here?
a not to smoke *b* if you don't smoke *c* not smoking *d* if I smoke

24 He has no parents. He is … .
a an only child *b* an orphan *c* unique *d* a loner

25 I am not used to … on the left
a drive *b* driven *c* driving *d* drove

Accuracy building 2

Now complete the following statements from memory Do not look back at the previous exercise.

1 I'm not … of ghosts.
2 I thought he was a friend of … .
3 The fishing … set sail at dawn.
4 He didn't get home until … after dark.
5 The cat scratched me with its … .
6 I still like him … his quick temper.
7 Smoking is known to … your health.
8 Be careful or you'll … over the dog crossing the road.
9 After the accident he lost his … of smell.
10 On 21 July 1969, Neil Armstrong set foot on the moon. That is a … .
11 He has decided to turn over a new …. He is determined to start afresh.
12 He is very unreliable. This is the second time he has let me … .
13 Be careful how you drive. The hill is very … .
14 He spent the whole day on the golf … .
15 There have been many great … in the history of medical science.
16 I went to see my doctor for a … .
17 These houses are very old, … from around the sixteenth century.
18 They are … to be still alive and the search for them will continue.
19 She acquired a beautiful sun … during her two weeks in Greece.
20 He … horses for export.
21 I haven't heard … my brother for ages.
22 There is no need to … your voice. I am not deaf, you know!
23 Would you mind … until we have finished eating?
24 He is an … . His parents died in a car accident.
25 You'll soon get used to … on the left.

4

Spotlight on conditionals

Finish each sentence in such a way that it means exactly the same as the sentence above it.

He didn't hurry, so he missed the train.
If he had hurried, *he wouldn't have missed the train.*

1 Be back by eleven o' clock or I shall be very angry.
I shall … .

2 Unless you leave straightaway, you'll be late for your appointment.
If … .

3 If we do not receive the goods by Friday, we shall cancel the order.
Unless … .

4 I'll only do it if you promise not to tell anybody.
I won't … .

5 Should you see Fred, please tell him to get in touch with me.
If … .

6 I advise you to buy the house now before the price goes up.
If I … .

7 You'd better not tell her about it.
If I … .

8 I know that you are not really a policeman because you haven't got any form of identification.
If you … .

9 You find the work difficult because you do not pay enough attention in class.
If … .

10 She can't go to the party because she has got flu.
If … .

11 I don't know his address, so I can't post it to him.
If … .

12 Were I a few years younger, I would apply for that job.
If … .

13 I shouted at him because he was very rude to me.
If he … .

14 The service was bad, so we didn't leave a tip.
If … .

15 It was raining, so we didn't go out.
If … .

16 He didn't hear them come in because he was listening to some music.
If … .

17 I didn't have time to make you a birthday cake.
If … .

18 Had I known that he was going to be there, I would not have gone.
If … .

19 You didn't listen to my advice and now you are in trouble.
If … .

20 You have a splitting headache this morning because you drank too much last night.
If … .

Spotlight on adverbs

Complete each statement with the adverbial form of the adjective in the right-hand column. Some words are both adjectives and adverbs, and so will not need to be changed.

1	He always drives … .	slow
2	She likes to drive … .	fast
3	He is an … careful driver.	extreme
4	Please drive … .	careful
5	I am … sorry.	dreadful
6	You speak English … .	good
7	That was … stupid of you!	incredible
8	It's … done.	easy
9	It's … cheap.	fantastic
10	You are not thinking … .	logic
11	You worked … and deserve your success.	hard
12	She reacted … to the news.	angry
13	It rained … last night.	heavy
14	He arrived … .	late
15	She broke the news to him as … as possible.	gentle

Have a laugh

A priest was teaching a group of children the difference between right and wrong, honesty and dishonesty. He asked one boy: 'If you found a five-pound note lying on the pavement, would you keep it?'
The little boy thought for a moment and said, 'Oh no, Father, I wouldn't keep it.'
The priest was pleased with the reply. 'Good boy. I am glad to hear it. Tell me. What would you do with it?'
'I'd spend it,' replied the boy.

Reading

Read the passage below. Following the passage, you will find five unfinished statements. Decide which of the alternatives, *a*, *b*, *c* or *d*, best completes each statement.

HIGH IN THE SKY

'You don't stop from the moment you take off until you land,' says Stephanie Hodge, a 23-year-old air stewardess. 'It is fun,' she adds, 'but being on your feet all day is hard work.' Flexibility and dedication are the qualities she considers most important. 'You have to like people and have an approachable nature.'

Stephanie spent five years with British Airways on the check-in desk before moving on to join the nine thousand strong cabin crew. This is now a common career route for stewardesses. Stephanie serves largely European flights, including domestic hops like Manchester. She is given her schedule for a period of thirty days in advance and has six days on then three days off. A *day* might mean two flights or could include a night stopover in a foreign city.

Before take-off cabin crew are told about passengers with special needs. 'Dressing' the aircraft means checking for tidiness and that safety equipment has not been interfered with. During the flight Stephanie is busy serving meals, drinks and selling dutyfree items. If the crew are staying overnight at the outbound destination they are given a generous allowance for eating out, one of the perks of the job.

The six weeks' training course covers safety equipment and procedures, including fire-fighting, jumping in and out of swimming pools and learning how to deal with life rafts and chutes. Passengers do occasionally give birth sky-high; medical training extends further than dealing with nosebleeds. Training also covers role-playing for dealing with awkward or difficult passengers.

There are strict uniform regulations. Good grooming is more important than physical beauty. Once trained, cabin crew are advised by a 'grooming centre' on how best to present themselves. British Airways favours employing staff with a mixture of ages, so some crew are in their forties and fifties.

For Stephanie, the best aspect of her job is 'the recognition you get for reassuring passengers who are nervous about flying.' The worst aspects of the job are 'air-traffic control problems and passengers who take it out on you.' What advice would she give to others? 'The job is not as glamorous as people think,' says Stephanie. 'There are times when there is a disturbance and people are being sick!'

(adapted from an article in the *Daily Telegraph*)

1 Stephanie Hodge
a has no time to put her feet up during a flight.
b serves long European flights.
c has been an air stewardess for at least five years.
d first spent five years at a desk in a British Airways office.

2 British Airways
a allows Stephanie to eat out when she is abroad.
b pays for all the meals Stephanie has when she is on duty.
c only employs good-looking people.
d insists that staff take pride in their appearance.

3 Stephanie
a never knows how long she might be away.
b knows how to deliver a baby.
c has been trained in parachute jumping.
d was given swimming lessons during her training.

4 After take-off, Stephanie spends most of her time
a tidying the aircraft and checking the safety equipment.
b attending to passengers with special needs.
c preparing meals for passengers and serving them drinks.
d attending to the needs of the passengers.

5 Stephanie
a does not consider her job to be very important.
b says that the image people have of her job does not correspond with reality.
c enjoys all aspects of her work.
d regards sick people as a nuisance.

Spotlight on vocabulary: work

Answer each question. Then discuss the difference between the words or phrases in italics. Give examples.

1 If you are employed by Mr Brown, is he your *employer* or *employee*?
2 When you apply for a job, do you fill in an *applicant* or *application form*?
3 If you want a teaching job, do you apply for a *teaching post* or *a teaching work*?
4 If somebody is totally incompetent, should that person *be appointed to a position of responsibility* or *be dismissed*?
5 If you have just been given a week's notice, does that mean you have been *sacked* or *promoted*?
6 Does a post become *vacancy* or *vacant*?
7 When applying for a job, do you have to give the names of two *supporters* or *referees*?
8 Are employers interested in your *qualification* or *qualifications*?
9 If a job requires initiative, does that mean you have to use your own *judgement* or *imagination*?
10 If you have a regular job, does that mean you have a *routine* or a *steady job*?
11 If you lose your job through no fault of your own, are you made *redundant* or *surplus*?
12 If you work overtime, do you receive *extra wages* or a *bonus* for the time you have worked?
13 The people you work with, are they your *compatriots* or *colleagues*?
14 Do you *make* or *do* business?
15 Does a lawyer charge a *fee* or a *reward* for his services?
16 On an application form you have to state what your present job is. Do you put down that information under the heading, *marital status* or *occupation*?
17 To work in another country, do you usually require a work *permission* or *permit*?
18 If you are unemployed, are you *out of work* or *off work*?
19 If you are looking for work, are you *seeking* or *searching employment*?
20 If somebody is work-shy, is that person *industrious* or *idle*?

Spotlight on prepositions

Complete each statement with *to*, *for* or *of*.

1 She is grateful ... him ... his support.
2 Would you care ... a cup of coffee?
3 The police suspect him ... the crime but they have no definite proof.
4 I am longing ... a cigarette.
5 I wonder what has happened ... him.
6 I wonder what has become ... her.
7 I have informed the staff ... my decision.
8 I am sorry ... inform you that your father is seriously ill.

9 I feel sorry ... him. He has suffered so much recently.
10 The boy was punished by his teacher ... being late.
11 I wouldn't dream ... doing such a thing!
12 I have arranged ... the plumber ... call tomorrow.
13 He has been very kind ... me.
14 That was very kind ... you.
15 Soap is used ... washing.

Spotlight on verbs

Supply the correct form and tense of the verbs in brackets.

55 Elton Road
London
S.W.12 3EJ
20th August 1990

Dear Bill,
Thank you again for the lovely time we (have) last weekend. It (be) very kind of you (invite) us (stay) with you in the country, and both Teresa and I thoroughly (enjoy) ourselves.
Unfortunately, when we (get) back home we (find) that our house (burgle). We now seriously (think) of (move) to the country, because this (be) the second time we (burgle). In any case, we (grow) tired of city life and we both (feel) that it (be) time we (make) a firm decision (leave) London once and for all.
We (be) grateful if you (be able) (send) us details of any properties for sale near where you (live). I (write) to you soon.
Best wishes,

Anthony

Spotlight on spelling

Study the words for a minute. Then read out a word to a partner. Ask him or her to spell the word aloud. Check his or her spelling.

angrily
application
cigarette
colleague
dismissed
employee
envious
flexibility
glamorous
initiative
occasionally
occupation
overhaul
qualifications
reassuring
receive
recognition
referee
suggestion
tidiness

Pause for thought

What is the origin of the phrase *to get the sack* or *to be sacked?*

To be sacked means *to be dismissed from employment*. The probable explanation of this term is that workmen carried the tools of their trade in a bag or sack, and wherever they worked they would take their bag with them. When their services were no longer required, they took up their bag of tools and departed to seek a job elsewhere.

4

Writing

A colleague at work has just retired. You have been asked to make a speech and to present a gift at his or her retirement party. (120 - 180 words)

Some useful phrases:
Ladies and gentlemen, we are gathered here ...
I have known ...
I can truthfully say ...
I am sure you will all agree when I say ...
I remember the time when ...
I shouldn't say this but ...
The office will never be the same without ...
We shall all miss ...
On behalf of the staff, I have great pleasure in presenting this ...
We hope this gift will remind you of ...
We wish you a happy retirement.

Exam tip

- Try to make the oral exam a pleasant experience, both for yourself and the examiner. Go into the examination room with a smile and try to sound enthusiastic when you speak.
- Look directly at the examiner as much as possible. Remember that you are speaking to the examiner, not to the photograph, the desk or the floor!
- Make sure that the examiner can actually hear what you are saying, especially if you are shy or have a very quiet voice. Above all, speak clearly and keep the examiner interested in what you are saying by varying the tone of your voice.

Speaking

1 Describe and comment on the girl's appearance.
2 Is it possible to tell what a person is like by the way that person dresses?
3 What factors influence your own choice of clothes? The price? Fashion? Comfort? Your friends? Your job?
4 If you were interviewing somebody for a job, would you pay much attention to what that person was wearing?
5 In what sort of clothes do you feel most comfortable when it is an extremely hot day? What sort of clothes do you usually wear on a bitterly cold day?

Unit 5

Accuracy building 1

Choose the most appropriate word or phrase to complete each statement. After deciding which is the correct answer, focus your attention on the alternatives. When can they be used?

1 I haven't seen her for … .
a ages *b* long time *c* long *d* while

2 Do you … in God?
a pray *b* worship *c* faith *d* believe

3 They are … to leave as soon as possible.
a worried *b* eagerly *c* anxious *d* wishing

4 The bank-robber was … to three years in prison.
a sent *b* judged *c* sentenced *d* convicted

5 I had just … out my washing to dry when it started to rain.
a hung *b* hanged *c* arranged *d* placed

6 There is no point … continuing this discussion.
a in *b* to *c* on *d* for

7 I wish to settle my account. To whom do I make … the cheque?
a up *b* out *c* for *d* up for

8 They burst … laughing when I told them what had happened.
a out *b* through *c* into *d* out of

9 Malaria is … by mosquitoes.
a translated *b* transmitted *c* transformed *d* transported

10 She's … research into the causes of cancer.
a making *b* carrying *c* doing *d* experimenting

11 The traditional English breakfast … of eggs, bacon, sausages and fried bread.
a comprises *b* composed *c* consists *d* contains

12 When we … in, we draw air into our lungs.
a breath *b* inhale *c* exhale *d* breathe

13 Don't forget to … your alarm for seven o'clock.
a set *b* wind *c* rewind *d* position

14 A public holiday in England is called a … holiday.
a Popular *b* Folk *c* Bank *d* Festival

15 Don't … of the rope!
a untie *b* release *c* unfasten *d* let go

16 There's nothing to it. It's a piece of … !
a bread *b* cake *c* furniture *d* paper

17 Last night Scotland … England by two goals to nil.
a won *b* gained *c* scored *d* beat

18 When approaching an airport, aircraft must contact the control tower for … to land.
a a permit *b* a licence *c* permission *d* an allowance

19 This is a non-smoking area. Please put … your cigarette.
a off *b* out *c* down *d* up

20 All birds reproduce by … eggs.
a lying *b* frying *c* scrambling *d* laying

21 The lens of a camera must be kept … clean.
a spotless *b* immaculate *c* spotlessly *d* dirt-free

22 … refreshments are available on this train.
a Soft *b* Light *c* Mild *d* Small

23 He has been drinking all evening and is as drunk as a … .
a judge *b* journalist *c* lord *d* pink elephant

24 The Great Wall of China is 1,500 miles … .
a wide *b* length *c* deep *d* long

25 Here's a bottle of wine. Has anybody got a … ?
a screwdriver *b* bottle-opener *c* corkscrew *d* tin-opener

Accuracy building 2

Now complete the following statements from memory. Do not look back at the previous exercise.

1 She hasn't written to me for … .
2 An atheist does not … in God.
3 He doesn't seem very … to meet her.
4 He was … to ten years in prison for his part in the robbery.
5 Why have you … the picture there? Wouldn't it look better over the mantelpiece?
6 I don't see any point … doing that.
7 The cheque should be made … to Bates Ltd.
8 The situation was so funny that we burst … laughing.
9 Many diseases are … by insects.
10 He's … research into the causes of skin disease.
11 A football team … of eleven players.
12 We take in oxygen when we … in.
13 I overslept this morning because I forgot to … my alarm clock.
14 Tomorrow is a … holiday.
15 … of my arm! You are hurting me.
16 Honestly, it's a piece of … !
17 West Germany … Brazil by three goals to one.
18 Who gave you … to smoke?
19 Fortunately the fire was quickly put … .
20 You can help your mother by … the table.
21 Their living-room is kept … clean.
22 … refreshments can be obtained during the interval.
23 Merry? I'd say he's as drunk as a … !
24 Their garden wall is thirty metres … .
25 It is difficult to open a bottle of wine without a … .

Spotlight on expressing preference

Finish each sentence in such a way that it means exactly the same as the sentence above it.

Do you prefer the green sweater or the red one?
Which sweater do you prefer,the green one or the red one?

1 I think the blue jumper is nicer than the red one.
I prefer ... .

2 She is keener on swimming than on jogging.
She prefers ... .

3 Let's leave tonight, not tomorrow morning.
I'd prefer ... .

4 They don't like the idea of travelling by coach. They'd prefer to go by train.
They'd rather ... .

5 She'd rather not talk about it.
She'd prefer ... .

6 Please don't mention this to anyone.
I'd rather you ... .

7 We'd prefer you not to visit her just yet.
We'd rather ... .

8 I'd prefer him to paint the kitchen first.
I'd rather ... .

9 I'd prefer the work to be done by a professional builder.
I'd rather ... .

10 He'd rather go to prison than pay the fine.
He'd sooner ... .

Spotlight on relative pronouns

Complete each statement with *who, whom, whose, that* or *which*. More than one alternative may be possible. In which of the statements is it possible to omit the relative pronoun?

1 That's the man ... stole her purse.
2 That's the woman ... purse was stolen.
3 Soap is something ... we all use.
4 That's the bridge from ... he jumped to his death.
5 *Rumours*, ... I saw last week, is not a very good film.
6 If there's one thing ... annoys me it's people ... jump queues.
7 This is not the first time ... you have lied to me!
8 That man, ... is talking to the receptionist, is my brother.
9 My brother is a man ... everybody admires.
10 Is that the woman from ... you obtained the information?
11 Is there anything ... I can do for you?
12 Coal, ... is essential to industry, is going up in price.
13 Chess is a game ... I enjoy very much.
14 Hunting foxes is a sport of ... he thoroughly disapproves.
15 He says he hasn't got any money, ... is a lie.

5

Have a laugh

'Come on, Andrew,' said his mother. 'Hurry up or you'll be late for school.'
'I don't want to go to school,' said Andrew.
'But you must,' insisted his mother.
'The teachers all hate me, and I hate them,' moaned Andrew.
'Even so...,' began his mother.
'The children, don't like me and I don't like them either,' said Andrew.
'You still have to go,' said his mother.
'But why must I?' he asked, his eyes filling with tears.
'Well,' replied his mother, 'first of all, you are fifty years old, and secondly, you are the headmaster of the school ... .'

Reading

Read the passage below. Following the passage, you will find five unfinished statements. Decide which of the alternatives, *a*, *b*, *c* or *d*, best completes each statement.

TRAGEDY AT SEA

Three members of the crew of a French trawler were drowned yesterday and a fourth was presumed dead after their vessel capsized thirty miles off the Sussex coast when, it is understood, its nets were caught on a wreck on the sea bed.

A major rescue operation, co-ordinated by coastguards and involving divers, helicopters, lifeboats and other fishing vessels, was launched when the French trawler was found floating upturned by the British trawler *Seabreeze 2*.

Two members of the crew were rescued from the sea, one by a coastguard helicopter, the other by the French trawler *Port Manek*, which had joined the search and which later recovered a body. The survivors were flown to hospital in Brighton where one of them is in a serious condition. Divers from the Royal Navy diving centre at Portland recovered two other bodies from inside the vessel. At first it was thought that only five men had been aboard the vessel but one of the two survivors told rescuers that there had been a crew of six.

Solent coastguards, who are still co-ordinating the search for the missing sixth crew member, say the 50ft vessel is floating upside down in the water and is fixed in the same position because its nets are trapped on the sea bed.

The shipping maritime accident investigation branch of the Department of Transport has been informed of the accident and will begin investigations today. A coastguard spokesman said they would concentrate the inquiry on whether the vessel was pulled over after getting its nets caught on a wreck.

'It is too soon to speculate as to exactly what happened, but this is a definite possibility. The nets are trapped on a sea bed obstacle though what it is at this stage, we don't know,' the spokesman said. 'The trawler was still fixed to the sea bed by its trawling nets when we reached it, and that gave us a good marking point to work from. There is still one man missing but hopes for his survival are fading.'

The air and sea rescue operation was launched by the coastguard after *Seabreeze 2* discovered the upturned hull shortly after 7 am yesterday. Two coastguard helicopters and a lifeboat were scrambled and joined by five other vessels in a search for survivors. The two surviving crew members were found floating three miles away from their vessel shortly before noon.

(from a report in *The Times*)

1 The two survivors were rescued
a because they had remained close to their capsized vessel.
b about five hours after the rescue operation was launched.
c by a French trawler.
d from the sea and shortly after 7 am.

2 The trawler
a is now trapped on the sea bed.
b capsized because it hit a wrecked ship.
c is drifting upside down in the sea.
d has remained in a fixed position since the accident.

3 The bodies of the drowned crew members were recovered
a from inside the capsized vessel.
b by Royal Navy divers.
c by fishermen and divers.
d by the British trawler, *Seabreeze 2*.

4 A sixth crew member
a is also known to have drowned.
b is now known to have been on board the trawler.
c is thought to be missing.
d is probably still alive,which is why the search for him is continuing.

5 At this stage, it is only known for certain that
a the two survivors are in a serious condition.
b the vessel was pulled over after getting its nets caught on a wreck on the sea bed.
c a lifeboat took the two survivors to hospital.
d the trawler's nets are trapped on some kind of sea bed obstacle.

Spotlight on vocabulary: water transport

Answer each question. Then discuss the difference between the words or phrases in italics. Give examples.

1 Would you describe a journey by ship as a *voyage* or a *ride*?
2 When people go on a sea cruise, do they usually travel on a *tanker* or a *liner*?
3 Is the stretch of water between England and France called the English *Channel* or *Canal*?
4 Do you row a boat by means of *oars* or *paddles*?
5 Mr Brown would like to buy a luxury boat. Would he buy a *canoe* or a *yacht*?
6 Is it quicker to cross the English Channel by *ferry* or *hovercraft*?
7 If you are a seaman, are you a *soldier* or a *sailor*?
8 Do you *drive* or *steer* a boat?
9 Does a ship usually set sail at *low tide* or at *high tide*?
10 If you are in a canoe on a river, is it easier to travel *upstream* or *downstream*?
11 Does a river *flow* or *circulate*?
12 Who would be in charge of a fleet of warships, a *captain* or an *admiral*?
13 If a ship sends out an SOS signal, is it *in port* or *in distress*?
14 Where would the captain of a ship sleep, *in his cabin* or *on the deck*?
15 If you are on a boat in mid-Atlantic, are you *at sea* or *in the sea*?
16 Do you find *waves* or *puddles* on the surface of the sea?
17 What is the land along the edge of a river called, the river *shore* or *bank*?
18 Are you more likely to find a *tug-boat* or a *barge* on a canal?
19 Are you more likely to be sea-sick during a *smooth crossing* or *when the sea is rough*?
20 Do *dockers* or *dustmen* unload a ship's cargo?

5

Spotlight on prepositions

Complete each statement with *in, on, of, off, with* or *for.*

1 We can rely ... him.
2 What do they have ... common?
3 He had difficulty ... making himself understood.
4 It is difficult ... me to make a decision.
5 The ship is bound ... New York.
6 His leg is ... plaster.
7 Take no notice ... her.
8 Who has not heard ... Shakespeare?
9 He was knocked ... his bicycle.
10 She was accused ... murder.
11 She was charged ... murder.
12 She was a woman ... great beauty.
13 Do you see that man ... long hair? I'm sure I've seen him ... television.
14 He is ... medium height and average build.
15 I have been robbed ... all my jewellery.

Spotlight on verbs

Complete the story below with the correct form and tense of the verbs in brackets.

Some months ago three rather absent-minded university professors (arrive) at a station just as the last train of the day (be) about (leave). They (run) to the platform where the train already (move) slowly out of the station.
'Quick!' (shout) one of the professors. He (succeed) in (open) one of the carriage doors, and two of them (manage) (jump) aboard. The third, however, (slip) and (fall) flat on the platform.
The train (disappear), and a porter (hurry) over to the professor who (lie) on the ground. (Help) the professor to his feet, the porter (ask) him : 'You (hurt) yourself?'
'No, I (be) fine. I (not break) anything.'
'Well, at least your two friends (catch) the train,' (say) the porter.
'But I (not think) they (be) very happy when they (realise) what they (do),' (reply) the professor,(shake) his head. 'They only (come) to the station (see) me off!'

Pause for thought

Why do we say *bless you* after someone has sneezed?

Bless you is short for *God bless you*, which means *May God protect you and bring you good fortune.*

According to one story, the saying started with St Gregory (328 – 390 AD), who used to say it during a terrible plague. The plague was a dreadful disease transmitted by rats, and there was no cure for it. The first symptom of this fatal disease was a sneeze. So if you started sneezing during the time of a plague, it was almost certain that you would die a horrible death.

5

Spotlight on spelling

Study the words for a minute. Then read out a word to a partner. Ask him or her to spell the word aloud. Check his or her spelling.

anxious	mantelpiece
available	permission
breathe	professional
captain	queue
disappear	receptionist
disease	rescue
essential	research
jewellery	serious
launched	survivor
laughing	transmitted

Writing

You have just returned from a package holiday abroad. It was not an enjoyable experience. Write a letter of complaint to the tour operator. (120 – 180 words)

Remember:

- that you are writing a formal letter.
- to write the name (if known) and position of the person you are writing to,together with the name and address of the company, on the left of the page above your opening.
- to end the letter with *Yours faithfully* if your opening is *Dear Sir* or *Dear Madam.*
- to end the letter with *Yours sincerely* if your opening is *Dear Mr, Mrs* or *Ms.*
- that *I look forward to* is more formal than *I am looking forward to.*

Some useful phrases:

I am writing to complain ...	*We were told that we would be staying ...*
First of all ...	*When we arrived, we found ...*
Furthermore ...	*To my horror, I discovered ...*
Moreover ...	*I could hardly believe my eyes when ...*
What's more ...	*Unless I receive a full refund within ...*
Finally ...	*I wish to claim compensation for ...*
Your brochure stated that ...	*I should be grateful if you would ...*
Nobody told us ...	*Thanking you for your kind attention.*

Exam tip

- It is important to remember that the oral exam is an interview, and that you are required to do more than just give a mechanical response however correct, to each question. Every time you are asked a question, the examiner is giving you an opportunity to start some form of conversation.

- It is equally important to remember that, unlike a written exercise, there is no 'right' or 'wrong' answer to an oral question. The examiner will ask you questions in order to listen to your response. Even if you do not know the actual answer to a particular question, you can still respond in a way that will gain you good marks. The object of the exercise is to see whether you can express yourself in English.

5

Speaking

1 Are the men in the photograph fishermen or anglers? What is the difference?
2 What sort of equipment are the men using? What is the simplest way of catching a fish?
3 Do you consider fishing to be an interesting hobby, a cruel sport or just a waste of time?
4 How often do you eat fish? Do you prefer fish to meat? Some doctors say that everybody should eat more fish and less meat. Do you agree?
5 If somebody says to you, 'that sounds fishy' or 'that's a fishy story', what do you think that person means?

Unit 6

Accuracy building 1

Choose the most appropriate word or phrase to complete each statement. After deciding which is the correct answer, focus your attention on the alternatives. When can they be used?

1 Perhaps we'll go for a picnic tomorrow. It all depends … the weather.
a of *b* about *c* on *d* with

2 We could tell she was surprised by the … on her face.
a sight *b* looking *c* appearance *d* expression

3 The sweater will … if you wash it in boiling water.
a shrink *b* reduce *c* fade *d* melt

4 I'll let you … this time, but don't do it again.
a down *b* out *c* off *d* in

5 My watch has gone. Someone must … it.
a take *b* be taking *c* have taken *d* took

6 I suggest we … at six this evening.
a to meet *b* will meet *c* are meeting *d* meet

7 The sun … in the east and sets in the west.
a raises *b* arouses *c* rises *d* arises

8 There has been a great … of discussion about how to tackle the problem.
a deal *b* lot *c* number *d* quantity

9 It weighs practically nothing. It's as light as a … .
a leaf *b* petal *c* snowflake *d* feather

10 Would passengers for flight number BA 203 please proceed to boarding … 15.
a card *b* gate *c* house *d* school

11 It's not unusual to see people … home drunk after a night out at the pub.
a striding *b* trampling *c* staggering *d* treading

12 You can … his surprise when he heard the news.
a suppose *b* see *c* wonder *d* imagine

13 The river burst its banks and … the surrounding area.
a watered *b* flooded *c* soaked *d* sprinkled

14 He … often go for a swim in the lake when he was a child.
a would *b* used *c* tended *d* accustomed

15 Your hands are … . Go and wash them at once.
a rotten *b* filthy *c* nasty *d* awful

16 She has … her heart on going to the USA.
a given *b* crossed *c* set *d* broken

17 The milk smells funny. I think it's … .
a mouldy *b* stale *c* rancid *d* off

18 The trouble with buying things on credit is the amount of … you have to pay per month.
a loan *b* interest *c* debit *d* debt

19 He was … when he heard the astonishing news.
a speechless *b* tongue-tied *c* helpless *d* dumb

20 The fire … out at four o'clock in the morning.
a started *b* broke *c* burst *d* spread

21 He is keen … start straightaway.
a on *b* in *c* for *d* to

22 I've just been … by a bee.
a scratched *b* pricked *c* stung *d* bitten

23 He says in his letter that he … to return to London in the near future.
a will hope *b* may *c* hopes *d* is hopping

24 I … across some old diaries the other day while clearing out a cupboard.
a found *b* came *c* discovered *d* encountered

25 You should take an umbrella with you in case it … .
a rains *b* will rain *c* may rain *d* might rain.

Accuracy building 2

Now complete the following statements from memory. Do not look back at the previous exercise.

1 That depends entirely … you.
2 I could tell from the … on his face that he was not very happy about it.
3 If the water is too hot, the jumper will … in the wash.
4 The Magistrate let him … with just a warning.
5 He must … it. He was the only person in the room.
6 I suggest we … tonight at the usual place.
7 Rain falls and smoke … .
8 Why don't you ask Professor Smith? He knows a great … about the subject.
9 It's not heavy at all. It's as light as a … .
10 Don't forget to shut the garden … .
11 Here he comes, … home drunk as usual!
12 You can … how shocked she was when she heard the news.
13 The river overflowed and … the neighbouring fields.
14 I … often walk to work when I was younger.
15 Your clothes are … . Go and get changed immediately.
16 He has … his heart on winning the first prize.
17 I wouldn't drink that milk if I were you. It's definitely … .
18 You will have to pay 12% … per month.
19 I am … . I just don't know what to say.
20 The fire … out at about six o'clock this morning.
21 I am keen … get this business over with as soon as possible.
22 He's just been … by a bee.
23 She says in her letter that she … everybody's well.
24 I … across a beautiful statuette while clearing out the attic.
25 You'd better take your raincoat in case it … .

6

Spotlight on liking and disliking

Finish each sentence in such a way that it means exactly the same as the sentence above it.

I don't like them at all
I really *dislike them.*

1 He usually goes to the cinema at least twice a month.
He likes … .

2 The programme amused me.
I found … .

3 She didn't like the book.
She didn't think … .

4 I find his behaviour objectionable.
I object … .

5 She felt depressed after seeing the film.
The film … .

6 I'd rather not go out tonight.
I don't feel … .

7 I am dreading my next visit to the dentist's.
I am definitely not looking … .

8 His visit pleased her very much.
His visit gave … .

9 Such conduct doesn't meet his approval.
He … .

10 I don't like her at all. She is so arrogant.
I can't … .

11 She doesn't object to baby-sitting now and again.
She doesn't … .

12 He finds your work unsatisfactory.
He is … .

13 Nobody in the class likes him.
He is … .

14 She admires him a lot.
She is full … .

15 There was loud applause from the audience.
The audience … .

Have a laugh

It was the end of the school day and all the children had gone home except for one little boy. With tears in his eyes, the little boy told his kindergarten teacher that only one pair of boots was left in the cloakroom and they weren't his. The teacher searched under desks and in corners but could not find any other boots. Exhausted, she asked the boy, 'How can you be sure these boots aren't yours?'
'Mine had snow on them,' the little boy replied.

Spotlight on prefixes

Complete each statement with the correct prefix: *dis-, un-, im-, in-, il-* or *ir-*.

1 I'm afraid I am ...able to help you.
2 I'm certain he's telling the truth. He's ...capable of telling a lie.
3 He's a very ...honest businessman. He would even cheat his own mother.
4 There was no need for you to be so ...courteous.
5 I considered his remark to be ...polite and I told him so.
6 Being ill is an ...pleasant experience.

6

7 He can be very ...agreeable and most people avoid his company.
8 Your handwriting is ...legible.
9 Murder is ...legal.
10 This list is ...accurate. There are four items missing.
11 We are dismissing him because he has been ...loyal to the firm.
12 He is not a good teacher. He is too ...patient.
13 It was ...responsible of you to leave the children on their own.
14 I am sacking the new secretary because she is ...efficient and ...reliable.
15 They told me at the interview that I was too ...experienced for the job.
16 I am ...familiar with this type of machine. Do you have a technical manual?
17 Long hair for men is ...fashionable these days.
18 Oh dear. How very ...fortunate!
19 I think you have been very ...kind to her.
20 Your work is ...satisfactory.

Spotlight on prepositions

Complete the following statements with *in, on, of, about, for, by* or *under*.

1 Think ... it and give me your decision tomorrow.
2 I can't think ... a solution to the problem.
3 I have often dreamt ... buying a cottage in the country.
4 May I pay ... cheque?
5 I'd rather you paid ... cash.
6 Don't worry. Everything is ... control.
7 ... no circumstances will I permit that to happen.
8 He charged me ten pounds ... cleaning the windows.
9 It was done ... error; not ... purpose.
10 She lives ... her own.
11 He prefers to go to the cinema ... himself.
12 I'm afraid it is not possible ... me to attend the meeting.
13 I hope they will not take advantage ... the situation.
14 There is no shame ... admitting that you were wrong.
15 You ought to be ashamed ... yourself.

Reading

Read the passage below. Following the passage, you will find five unfinished statements. Decide which of the alternatives, *a, b, c* or *d,* best completes each statement.

KEEP ON RUNNING

The New Zealand Olympic gold medallist John Walker is one of the best runners in the world. He has run more sub-four minute miles than anyone else ever. 'I went anywhere and everywhere, whenever I was asked to run to complete the record 100. Now I've run 127 of them. My next and last ambition in athletics is to run the sub-four minute mile at forty. No-one has done that.'

At 'almost forty', as he describes himself, by most standards John Walker would be over the hill. But he is a superb athlete, whose endurance and stamina are as legendary as his will to win. Those qualities have given him the world mile record in 1975 with a time of 3 minutes 49.4 seconds, several hundred victories, a Gold Medal at the 1976 Olympics, and on February 17,1985 he was the first man to run 100 sub-four minute miles.

'Doing the sub-four minute mile at forty will give me another first. At 37 I am beginning to get into years where no other runner has been,' he says, smiling wryly. 'I was 21 when I became serious about running. I was 24 when I became an Olympic gold medallist. A myth has grown up around me because I've been doing it for so long.

I train every day of my life. My only break comes for about three weeks after the races finish at the end of August,' says John. 'If I don't train that way, I fall apart very quickly. Muscle goes to fat very fast. Your body is like a machine, you have to maintain it. Running demands efficiency, talent and the right state of mind. Running conditions your heart and lungs, making them more efficient. I literally have a big heart, with a high lung capacity.

When I am at home on my ranch in New Zealand, I run five miles in the morning, between eight-forty and nine-thirty, then I mend the fences, train the ponies, arrange for the blacksmiths and clean out the horse boxes. Then I run another ten to fifteen six-minute miles. I play tennis when I can, and actually set out to be a tennis player in the first place.

Running is stress-related, because of the pounding on the legs,' explains John. 'I've had leg injuries and I know when to rest. The body tells you not to run. I can control nerves before a race because I focus on what I have to do. I don't get distracted.

I have a massage as often as I can, and I once went to a faith healer for a back injury. He cured an illness the surgeons could not, in two days. I could not believe it. But after that I don't pooh-pooh anything.

I have no particular diet, just healthy foods. I eat lots of vegetables and chicken, but I don't eat much red meat. I like the odd portion of fish and chips, and pizza. But athletes are usually not finicky. They run because they are good, not because of what they eat. My advice is balance, not fads.'

(adapted from an article in the *Daily Express*)

1 John Walker's ultimate ambition is
a to be the first person to run a sub-four minute mile.
b to be the first forty-year-old to run a sub-four minute mile.
c to run more sub-four minute miles than anyone else.
d to be the first forty-year-old to break the world mile record.

2 John Walker
a has won several hundred races.
b didn't take sport seriously until he was twenty-one.
c ran 100 sub-four minute miles in 1985.
d won an Olympic gold medal the year before he became a world-record holder.

3 When at home in New Zealand, John Walker
a runs twenty miles every day.
b devotes most of his time to running.
c keeps to a routine of regular runs, hard physical work and regular games of tennis.
d works on his ranch while maintaining his training schedule.

4 According to John Walker, a runner has to train his body to be as efficient as possible. He also says that
a running increases the size and capacity of one's heart and lungs.
b natural ability and the right attitude of mind are just as important.
c running demands total dedication and the right temperament.
d running requires the right technique and the will to win.

5 John Walker
a keeps to a strict diet of healthy foods.
b does not believe in faith healers.
c knows when to take things easy.
d regularly eats portions of fish and chips, and pizza.

6

Spotlight on vocabulary: sport

Answer each question. Then discuss the difference between the words or phrases in italics. Give examples.

1 Is football played on a *pitch* or a *track*?
2 If you are watching a game of football, are you a *viewer* or a *spectator*?
3 If you are playing football and you deliberately trip a player over, is that a *foul* or a *penalty*?
4 Does a *coach* or a *referee* take charge of training sessions?
5 Tom used to play tennis regularly but he has not played for the last two years. Is he out of *practice* or *practise*?
6 When playing tennis, do you hit the ball over a *net* or a *court*?
7 In table tennis, is the ball hit with a *racket* or a *bat*?
8 Is squash an *indoor* or an *outdoor* sport?
9 Is golf played with a *club* or a *stick*?
10 On which part of a bicycle does a cyclist sit, the *saddle* or the *handlebars*?
11 Do you take *place* or *part* in a race?
12 Does a jockey encourage a horse to run faster by means of the *reins* or *by using a whip*?
13 Do boxers fight in a *rink* or a *ring*?
14 Do you shoot at a *target* or an *aim*?
15 Do you shoot arrows with a *rifle* or a *bow*?
16 What do athletes usually wear when they are on a training run or warming up before a race, a *waistcoat* or a *tracksuit*?
17 Is a rugby ball *round* or *oval*?
18 Do you ski down a *cliff* or a *slope*?
19 If you are an enthusiastic supporter of some sport, are you a *fan* or a *hooligan*?
20 Can an athlete be *disqualified* or *disallowed* from an event?

Pause for thought

The English are well-known for their fish and chips. What is the origin of the word *chips*?

A chip is a very thin piece of wood that has come off a larger block of wood. When we want to say that a son is like his father, we say: *He's a chip off the old block.*

A *chip* is also a very thin piece of glass or porcelain that has come off the edge of a receptacle. If, for example, a small piece has come off the edge of a cup, we say that the cup is *chipped.* Thus when we cut a whole potato into much smaller pieces or slices, those thin pieces are called *chips.*

Chip is a very useful word and it is used in many different contexts. For example, a microcomputer comprising a microprocessor and memory can be integrated onto a single *chip* or slice of silicon about 5mm square and 1mm thick. Such a computer is known as a *single-chip* microcomputer.

6

Spotlight on verbs

Complete the letter below with the correct form and tense of the verbs in brackets.

56 Linton Grove
London
SE4 8AG
17th January 1990

Dear Cynthia,
Thank you for your letter which I (receive) this morning. It (be) lovely (hear) from you again after so many years. How long it (be) since we last (write) to each other? Five years? Six? Anyway, I (be) so glad that you (decide) (get) in touch with your old friends again.
You (say) in your letter that you (be) now married and that you (expect) your first child in June. Lucky you! I still (go) out with Roy - you (remember) him? We (go) out for more than seven years now, and he still (not ask) me (marry) him! He (keep) (tell) me he (love) me, but I (begin) (have) my doubts. What you (do) if you (be) in my position?
Anyway, we (have) plenty of time (talk) about such things next week when you (come) down to London. I really (look) forward (see) you again and, of course, I (die) (meet) your husband!
You (ask) in your letter whether Saturday (be) a convenient day for us (meet). No problem! Just (give) me a ring as soon as you (arrive) at your hotel.
All the best and lots of love,

Mary

Spotlight on spelling

Study the words for a minute. Then read out a word to a partner. Ask him or her to spell the word aloud. Check his or her spelling.

applause	discourteous	irresponsible	qualities
arrogant	exhausted	maintaining	regularly
audience	February	neighbouring	schedule
cloakroom	forty	objectionable	staggering
depressed	injuries	practically	surrounding

Writing

A friend of yours is coming to stay with you for a few days. Write a letter to your friend, apologising for the fact that you cannot meet him or her at the station or airport. Explain to your friend how to get to your house from the station or airport. (120-180 words)

Some useful phrases :
The best way to get to my house is to ...
When you come out of the station, cross the road and ...
There is a bus stop at the end of ...
Any bus will take you as far as ...
Make sure you get off at ...
The journey takes about ...
Take the first turning on the right ...
Keep straight on for about two hundred yards ...
Go past the traffic lights and then ...
Carry straight on until you come to ...

6

Exam tip

- You should prepare for the oral exam by practising speaking as much as possible, but you should not try to prepare fixed answers for set situations. Examiners are trained to spot students who are simply reciting phrases they have learnt by heart. You should be aware that you will be penalised if your answer is not a natural response.
- The interview is the one section of the exam that has to be approached in a spontaneous manner.

Speaking

1 What have the men in the photograph just done? What are they doing? What will happen soon?
2 Do you think that sky-diving is a particularly dangerous sport or a relatively safe one?
3 Why do you think some people prefer leisure activities that have some element of danger?
4 Describe any other leisure activity which you consider to be quite dangerous.
5 How do you spend your leisure time?

Unit 7

Accuracy building 1

Choose the most appropriate word or phrase to complete each statement. After deciding which is the correct answer, focus your attention on the alternatives. When can they be used?

1 He complained of severe … in his chest.
a hurt *b* ache *c* pain *d* injury

2 I … on seeing the manager.
a insist *b* demand *c* persist *d* request

3 All of a sudden, we were attacked by a … of bees.
a hive *b* swarm *c* herd *d* pack

4 You are not … to swim in this lake.
a let *b* supposing *c* admitted *d* allowed

5 'I don't like spinach.' '… !'
a I don't neither *b* So do I *c* I don't too *d* Nor do I

6 The sign is too far away. I can't make … what it says.
a out *b* clear *c* seen *d* visible

7 She wants … that she is sorry for what happened.
a that you know *b* you know *c* you to know *d* to know you

8 There's a strike on. There are no buses … today.
a running *b* working *c* functioning *d* driving

9 The burglar … into the room and started looking for jewellery and other items of value.
a crawled *b* shuffled *c* limped *d* crept

10 What have you … by doing that?
a succeeded *b* achieved *c* managed *d* accomplish

11 …! It's not the end of the world. I'm sure things will get better soon.
a Three cheers *b* Cheerio *c* Cheers *d* Cheer up

12 He was … two hundred pounds and disqualified from driving for six months.
a awarded *b* fined *c* charged *d* paid

13 The … on the motorway was really thick. It was like trying to see through a blanket!
a mist *b* haze *c* fog *d* steam

14 They offered me the job, but I decided to … it down.
a reject *b* turn *c* refuse *d* decline

15 Two firemen were … by the smoke and the heat.
a extinguished *b* died *c* overcome *d* collapsed

16 The box is too heavy for me to … .
a give a lift *b* lift it *c* lift *d* be lifted

17 A monk lives in a … .
a convent *b* church *c* cathedral *d* monastery

18 When the volcano … , the people in the village below fled for their lives.
a exploded *b* burst *c* erupted *d* blew up

19 The primary … of both tooth decay and gum disease is dental plaque.
a cause *b* reason *c* blame *d* fault

20 The tree was … by lightning.
a chopped down *b* fallen *c* struck *d* beaten

21 Crops grow best in … soil.
a barren *b* fertile *c* eroded *d* arid

22 The Olympic Games are … every four years.
a occurred *b* held *c* happening *d* played

23 Think of a number … one and ten.
a beside *b* below *c* among *d* between

24 The police are … into the matter.
a investigating *b* examining *c* looking *d* considering

25 I'd rather you … smoke, if you don't mind.
a don't *b* didn't *c* wouldn't *d* shouldn't

Accuracy building 2

Now complete the following statements from memory. Do not look back at the previous exercise.

1 Ever since the accident, he has suffered from constant … in his back.
2 I … on knowing the truth.
3 We were chased by a … of bees.
4 You are not … to fish in this river.
5 'I don't like phrasal verbs.' '… !'
6 Can you make … what it says?
7 She wants … that all is forgiven.
8 Owing to a derailment, many trains are … late this morning.
9 The burglar … up the stairs, hoping not to wake up the occupants of the house.
10 He has … the impossible.
11 Come on, … ! Every cloud has a silver lining.
12 She was … fifty pounds for parking on a double yellow line.
13 All planes have been grounded because of thick … on the runways.
14 It's a very good offer. I hope you are not going to … it down.
15 He was … by the fumes and had to be taken to hospital.
16 It weighs a ton! It's far too heavy for me to … .
17 He is a monk and has spent all his adult life in a … .
18 First there were earth tremors and then the volcano … .
19 The … of the accident is still a mystery to us.
20 The tower was … by lightning.
21 The land is so … that it invariably produces a rich harvest.
22 The meeting will be … at two o'clock in my office.
23 Arundel castle lies … London and Littlehampton.
24 They are … into the matter.
25 I'd rather you … swear in front of the children.

Spotlight on certainty, probability and possibility

Finish each sentence in such a way that it means exactly the same as the sentence above it.

I am absolutely certain. I have *no doubts at all.*

1 I am sure you are mistaken.
You must … .

2 I am sure he was joking.
He must … .

3 I am certain she hid it somewhere in this room.
She must … .

4 Somebody started the fire deliberately, of that I am certain.
The fire must … .

5 She definitely murdered her husband.
There is no … .

6 Are you sure there will not be any buses running tomorrow?
Is it … ?

7 There is no possibility of his signing that document.
I know for certain … .

8 Prices will almost certainly rise again within the next two months.
Prices are bound … .

9 I shall probably be late tomorrow.
It's quite likely … .

10 It will probably rain this afternoon.
It's likely … .

11 It's fairly certain that you will be promoted soon.
You are likely … .

12 There will probably be a lot of people there at that time of day.
There are likely … .

13 Surely she's not your mother! She looks far too young.
She can't … .

14 It would have been impossible for me to do it without your help.
I couldn't … .

15 I am sure he wasn't serious.
He can't … .

16 Perhaps somebody took it by mistake.
Somebody may … .

17 Mark might lend you the money. Why don't you ask him?
Perhaps … .

18 You might get lost, so take a map and compass with you.
Take … .

19 Take a warm coat as it might get cold tonight.
Take … .

20 There is a strong possibility that he will pass the exam.
He has a good chance … .

7

Spotlight on *as* and *like*

Complete each statement with *as* or *like*.

1 ... I mentioned in my last letter, we are unable to find the relevant documents.
2 ... you can see from this photo, the hotel was very near the sea.
3 He is ... his father in many ways.
4 You must make an effort, ... we all do, to get on with her.
5 The suspect is described ... being tall, fair-haired and broad-shouldered.
6 Last year, ... in 1989, the company made a huge profit.
7 He treats me ... if I were a ten-year-old!
8 He treats me ... a ten-year-old!
9 He is regarded ... the best in his field.
10 I like some school subjects, ... History and Geography.
11 There are some subjects, such ... French and Maths, which I don't like.
12 She works ... a chambermaid in a hotel.
13 It tastes ... rubber.
14 She is acting ... my guardian until my parents return.
15 He uses one of the bedrooms ... a study.
16 The cost of living has risen this year, ... it does every year.
17 Don't disturb the boss this morning. He's ... a bear with a sore head.

Have a laugh

Two explorers were walking through the jungle when suddenly a lion appeared in front of them. 'Keep calm,' said the first explorer. 'Just remember what we read in that book on wild animals. If you stand absolutely still and look a lion straight in the eye, he will turn tail and run away.' 'Fine,' said the second explorer. 'You've read the book. I've read the book. But has he read the book?'

Reading

Read the passage below. Following the passage, you will find five unfinished statements. Decide which of the alternatives, *a*, *b*, *c* or *d*, best completes each statement.

NOT SO PERFECT

One person, the American inventor Thomas Midgley (1889-1944), created what are considered to be two of today's biggest environmental evils : chlorofluorocarbons (CFCs) and leaded petrol.

His discoveries show how science can solve practical problems, but how seemingly perfect solutions can have disastrous consequences.

Shortly after the First World War, Midgley was searching for a chemical solution to the problem of an irritating knocking sound heard coming from car engines. This often occurs when the engine burns the fuel too quickly to use up all the power it is getting from it. Midgley found that the lead compound, tetraethyl lead, could help stop the knocking sound when it was used with the chemical bromine. He had developed the first leaded petrol which could be sold at American petrol stations.

Today, most scientists believe that lead released into the atmosphere from leaded petrol can cause brain damage in young children.

Midgley then turned his efforts to the refrigerator industry. One common way of cooling a fridge was by passing ammonia, mixed with water, through pipes which passed inside the fridge. If the mixture was pumped at different pressures, its temperature changed. The higher the pressure, the higher the temperature. But ammonia had leaked a number of times, and had harmed people. Midgley needed to find a safer substance. He developed the substance, chlorodifluoromethane, which is a CFC. This made refrigerators safer.

Scientists learned after Midgley's death in 1944 that CFCs were damaging the earth's ozone layer. By then, CFCs were considered so useful that they were widely used in pesticides. The household aerosol eventually became one of the largest users of the gases.

Sadly, another of Thomas Midgley's inventions had terrible consequences. In 1940 he was paralysed by polio, and he devised a harness and pulley system to help him get out of bed. In November 1944, he strangled himself while he was using it.

(from an article in *The Education Guardian*)

1 According to the passage,
a Midgley was a brilliant but evil scientist.
b Midgley's solutions to practical problems seemed perfect at the time.
c Midgley created the environmental problems we have today.
d Midgley's solutions to practical problems always involved chemicals.

2 Car engines used to burn fuel so fast that
a full use was not being made of the power that was generated.
b all the power from it was being used up too quickly.
c not enough power was being generated, which caused an irritating knocking sound.
d only an irritating knocking sound was produced.

3 We learn from the passage that
a before the development of CFCs, fridges were always cooled by pumping a mixture of ammonia and water through pipes which passed inside the fridge.
b ammonia has a tendency to leak through pipes because the hotter ammonia becomes, the more pressure it puts on the pipes.
c brain damage in young children is the result of lead in the atmosphere.
d a particular combination of chemicals made possible the development of leaded petrol.

4 CFCs
a are damaging the earth's surface.
b made household appliances safer than before.
c became widely used in sprays.
d may be polluting the earth's atmosphere.

5 Thomas Midgley
a committed suicide in November 1944.
b died as a consequence of one of his inventions.
c was unable to get out of bed for the last four years of his life.
d was paralysed after a terrible accident in 1940.

Exam tip

Learning vocabulary is not easy and you should be methodical in your approach.

- First of all, organize your vocabulary into particular subjects or themes.
- Secondly, divide any vocabulary list into two parts : active and passive. The active section will contain the words and phrases that you feel you need to learn by heart. The passive section will contain more difficult words and phrases, and these you should simply learn to recognise.
- The most important rule for effective vocabulary learning is that you should only learn by heart words and phrases that you know how to use. Active vocabulary is for communication. Passive vocabulary is for comprehension.

7

Spotlight on vocabulary: science and technology

Answer each question. Then discuss the difference between the words or phrases in italics. Give examples.

1 Does sugar *melt* or *dissolve* in hot water?
2 Does a piece of metal *expand* or *enlarge* when heated?
3 Does a sponge *digest* or *absorb* water?
4 Does a scientist work in a *laboratory* or a *lavatory*?
5 Does a scientist use *binoculars* or a *microscope* to examine very small objects?
6 Do scientists *carry off* or *carry out* experiments?
7 Is nylon a *synthetic* or a *toxic* fibre?
8 Do we usually *dig* or *drill* for oil?
9 In Great Britain, do cars run on *gas* or *petrol*?
10 Is the layer of gas round the earth known as the earth's *atmosphere* or *environment*?
11 When a satellite goes round the earth, is it in *orbit* or on a *roundabout*?
12 Do we *launch* or *land* rockets into space?
13 If an aircraft is travelling at supersonic speed, has it broken the *sound barrier* or *speed limit*?
14 Is a set of instructions for a computer called a *programme* or *program*?
15 Do computers process *hardware* or *data*?
16 Does a camera have a *lens* or a *magnifying glass*?
17 Does a television have a *screen* or a *windscreen*?
18 Do *meteorologists* or *geologists* forecast tomorrow's weather?
19 Is *psychology* or *ecology* the branch of science that looks at plants and animals in relation to the environment in which they live?
20 Is the movement of electricity along a conducting body known as an *electric current* or *radar*?

Spotlight on prepositions

Complete each statement with *in*, *on*, *to*, *for*, *between*, *of* or *with*.

1 She has already gone. She left ... Dover an hour ago.
2 Is there any difference ... 'to arrive at' and 'to get to'?
3 They provided me ... everything I needed.
4 His teachers are satisfied ... the progress he is making.
5 He was fined one hundred pounds ... being drunk and disorderly.
6 I am tired ... listening to your excuses.
7 That was very considerate ... her.
8 There is something wrong ... my car.
9 He has invested all his money ... stocks and shares.
10 He sometimes bets ... horses.
11 You ought to go ... a diet.
12 He tore the paper ... half.
13 They disapprove ... him.
14 Prepare yourself ... a shock.
15 Who were you speaking to ... the phone?

Spotlight on verbs

The following are all answers to particular questions. What do you think the questions were?

I am twenty-one.
How old are you?

1 I take size nine.
2 From platform number six.
3 No, but I'd like to go there one day. I have heard that the Scottish Highlands are beautiful.
4 No, of course not. Go ahead. It's rather stuffy in here.
5 Oh, about four years. I met him at a party and we have been good friends ever since.
6 Yes, he was about six feet tall with long curly hair. He was wearing jeans and a brown jumper.
7 John did, but it was an accident. He didn't do it on purpose.
8 Yes, here it is. You can see yesterday's date on it. Now, can I exchange this shirt for another one?
9 The town centre? Carry straight on down this road and take the second turning on the left.
10 Well, it's certainly better than my previous flat.
11 Yes, could you please tell him to give me a ring as soon as he gets in? He's got my number.
12 It's called a screwdriver.
13 Yes, I'll have the dish of the day.
14 That's very kind of you. Thank you.
15 Thank you very much. I'd love one.

Spotlight on spelling

Study the words for a minute. Then read out a word to a partner. Ask him or her to spell the word aloud. Check his or her spelling.

absolutely
atmosphere
brilliant
burglar
castle
collapsed
committed
consequences
current
difference
disastrous
dissolve
environment
irritating
magnifying
paralysed
temperature
tendency
terrible
travelling

Pause for thought

Is there any truth in the saying, *lightning never strikes in the same place twice*?

This popular saying is often used to reassure people who have suffered a misfortune. It is based, however, on wishful thinking and not on scientific fact. There have been many recorded instances of lightning striking the same spot twice. Perhaps the strangest case on record is the following:

In 1899, lightning struck a man dead in his back yard in Taranto, Italy. Thirty years later, his son was killed on the same spot and in the same manner. Then in 1949, a third man was killed in the same back yard – struck by lightning. He was the grandson of the first man and the son of the second man!

7

Writing

Imagine that you are a teacher and that you wish to explain to a group of children how they should behave when visiting the countryside. Explain why they should or should not do certain things. (120 – 180 words) Refer to the country code given below.

THE COUNTRY CODE

1 *Enjoy the countryside and respect its life and work.*
2 *Guard against all risk of fire.*
3 *Fasten all gates.*
4 *Keep your dogs under close control.*
5 *Keep to public paths across farmland.*
6 *Use gates and stiles to cross fences, hedges and walls.*
7 *Leave livestock, crops and machinery alone.*
8 *Take your litter home.*
9 *Help to keep all water clean.*
10 *Protect wildlife, plants and trees.*
11 *Take special care on country roads.*
12 *Make no unnecessary noise.*

Spotlight on pronunciation

Read out the following sentences, making sure that you pronounce each word correctly. Pay particular attention to the stress pattern of each word.

1 That's a nice photograph.
2 He is a professional photographer.
3 I am interested in photography.
4 There's an interesting advertisement in today's paper.
5 Most companies advertise their products.
6 I'm afraid we cannot give you a refund.
7 She is making sound progress.
8 In three hours we hardly progressed at all.
9 We import tea from India.
10 You will have to pay import duty on those cameras.
11 We need to increase production.
12 How can you justify such a large increase in price?
13 I always travel by public transport.
14 How are we going to transport these goods?
15 May I borrow your tape-recorder? I'd like to record some music.
16 They have sold one million copies of their latest record.
17 I am anxious to begin as soon as possible.
18 He caused her a great deal of anxiety.
19 There are various reasons for her strange behaviour.
20 There is a great variety to choose from.

Unit 8

Accuracy building 1

Choose the most appropriate word or phrase to complete each statement. After deciding which is the correct answer, focus your attention on the alternatives. When can they be used?

1 She says she is quite happy in her … job, but she still hasn't found what she really wants.
a actual *b* present *c* permanent *d* previous

2 I'll write … soon.
a you *b* to you *c* to you a letter *d* you a line

3 That was the most exciting … of football I have ever seen.
a game *b* match *c* play *d* show

4 Flight A509 from New York is … to arrive at nine o'clock.
a planned *b* bound *c* due *d* expecting

5 Can you put me … for the night?
a off *b* through *c* away *d* up

6 She … after her mother. They have the same temperament.
a takes *b* looks *c* seems *d* appears

7 I was taken completely … surprise.
a at *b* in *c* to *d* by

8 The matter is urgent. Please reply by … of post.
a telex *b* registered *c* first *d* return

9 He's … mad.
a jumping *b* leaping *c* hopping *d* skipping

10 I'm tired. I think I'll take a … .
a napkin *b* nappy *c* nap *d* nape

11 She has to go up four … of stairs to reach her flat.
a flights *b* landings *c* cases *d* steps

12 I keep … my glasses. I never seem able to find them when I need them.
a misleading *b* mislaying *c* mishandling *d* missing

13 Add the chocolate to the milk and … well.
a wind *b* stir *c* spin *d* twist

14 Politicians have to … many speeches.
a do *b* tell *c* make *d* say

15 How would you like your steak, …, medium or well-done?
a rare *b* raw *c* crude *d* natural

16 He has … his ankle.
a wounded *b* injury *c* sprained *d* swollen

17 He gave a … of relief and said, 'I'm glad that's over'.
a sigh *b* sign *c* gesture *d* blow

18 She … fair-haired.
a has *b* prefers *c* is *d* possesses

19 I need your support. I hope you will back me ... at the next meeting.
a out *b* into *c* down *d* up

20 Peter was made ... in 1985 and has not worked since.
a sacked *b* unemployment *c* dismissed *d* redundant

21 Cycling is ... the most popular means of transport in the world.
a doubtfully *b* with doubt *c* undoubtedly *d* in doubt

22 I ... saw Michael two years ago.
a last *b* last time *c* the last time *d* lastly

23 I'll ... the lawn this afternoon.
a trim *b* prune *c* chop *d* mow

24 I think we have done enough work. Let's call it ... .
a off *b* a day *c* evens *d* quits

25 We've got an hour to ... before the film starts. What shall we do?
a kill *b* waste *c* lose *d* spend

Accuracy building 2

Now complete the following statements from memory. Do not look back at the previous exercise.

1 There are no vacancies at ... .
2 Has she written ... since she left England?
3 I didn't enjoy that ... of football.
4 The train is ... to arrive at seven o'clock.
5 Some friends put me ... for the night.
6 He ... after his father. They are similar in so many ways.
7 It was totally unexpected. She was taken completely ... surprise.
8 I would appreciate a reply by ... of post.
9 I've never seen him so angry. He's ... mad!
10 You look exhausted. Why don't you take a ... ?
11 The lift is not working and I don't fancy climbing fifteen ... of stairs!
12 He keeps ... his lighter. He can never remember where he has left it.
13 You should ... the soup every few minutes.
14 I have to ... a very important speech tonight.
15 I prefer my steak ..., not medium or well-done.
16 He has ... his wrist and will not be able to play tennis for a week or so.
17 She gave a ... of contentment and hugged her baby again.
18 She ... broken-hearted.
19 Don't worry, I'll back you ... .
20 Two hundred workers have been made ... .
21 She is ... the best teacher this school has ever had.
22 I can't remember when I ... saw such a funny film.
23 It takes me about twenty minutes to ... the lawn.
24 I'm exhausted. Let's call it ... .
25 We've arrived too early. We've got about an hour to ... .

8

Spotlight on wishing, regretting and apologising

Finish each sentence in such a way that it means exactly the same as the sentence above it.

I'm sorry I'm late. He apologised *for arriving late.*

1 What a pity Michael can't come with us.
I wish ... .

2 It's a pity I can't speak French.
I wish ... .

3 Betty has to go to school even though she doesn't want to.
Betty wishes ... .

4 The area I live in is not very nice.
I wish I ... .

5 Please don't keep interrupting me!
I wish you ... .

6 Please stop arguing!
I wish you ... .

7 I regret not learning to play the guitar when I was younger.
I wish ... .

8 I regret buying the car.
I wish ... .

9 They would like to book a room for the night.
They wish ... .

10 It's a pity I haven't got any money on me.
If only ... .

11 It's a pity it's still raining.
If only ... .

12 You should have told me earlier.
If only ... .

13 It was wrong of me not to inform you.
I ought ... .

14 I am sorry to disturb you so late at night, but the matter is rather urgent.
I apologise ... .

15 I think you ought to tell her that you are sorry.
I think you ought to ... .

16 'I'm sorry I was rude to you last night,' said Andrew to Mary.
Andrew apologised ... .

17 You should make him apologise.
You should ask him for ... .

18 I do apologise for having kept you waiting.
I am sorry ... .

19 We very much regret any inconvenience that the delay may have caused.
We are sorry ... .

20 I'm sorry, the hotel is full.
The hotel ... .

8

Spotlight on the definite article

In some of the following sentences the definite article has been omitted. Correct any sentence which is grammatically wrong by adding *the* where appropriate.

1 She had an accident and had to be taken to hospital.
2 What is name of hospital she was taken to?
3 Hurry up or you'll be late for school.
4 She was ill and didn't go to school for a week.
5 I'd like to send my son to school your children attend.
6 Doctor told her to stay in bed for a few days.
7 He found some money under bed.
8 And who is going to make beds? I'm certainly not going to!
9 Most people are kind to animals.
10 Most of people in room were non-smokers.
11 People who live next door to us are very nice.
12 She plays piano.
13 What do you normally have for breakfast?
14 Intelligence is more important than beauty.
15 What do you think is greatest discovery made by man?
16 I always drink white wine on social occasions.
17 I didn't think much of wine they served us last night.
18 Foreigners often make jokes about British weather.
19 What horrible weather!
20 Experts claim that fish is healthier than meat.

Have a laugh

A man went for a brain transplant and was offered the choice of two brains – an architect's for £100 and a politician's for £10,000.
'Does that mean the politician's brain is much better than the architect's?' asked the man.
'Not exactly,' replied the brain transplant salesman. 'It's just that the politician's brain has never been used.'

Reading

Read the passage below. Following the passage, you will find five unfinished statements. Decide which of the alternatives, *a*, *b*, *c* or *d*, best completes each statement.

DAYLIGHT ROBBERY

Three paintings worth at least £10 million were stolen yesterday in London from beneath the noses of Britain's leading lawyers. The thief grabbed all three works of art from the Great Hall of Lincoln's Inn, the traditional dining place of the legal profession.

Police had repeatedly warned about poor security at Lincoln's Inn, which does not even have an alarm system. Only a gatekeeper, whose main job is to watch for illegally parked cars, was on duty when the raider drove up to the entrance to Lincoln's Inn in broad daylight at 5.30 pm.

As the gatekeeper came out to question him, the man beat him to the ground knocking him unconscious. The gatekeeper was dragged inside the building and his hands were tied behind his back. The thief stole the gatekeeper's keys, let himself into the Great Hall and expertly cut the masterpieces out of their frames. He is believed to have got away in a red Ford Escort car. The whole raid took less than fifteen minutes.

A police spokesman said : 'This was a daring raid carried out by a man who knew exactly what he was doing. The paintings were expertly cut out, and it takes great skill to do that.'

The haul is believed to have been stolen to order for a wealthy collector, and there is little chance of getting any of it back.

Detectives from Holborn police station sealed off the area and passers-by were quizzed as to whether they had seen anyone hanging around in a suspicious manner. The injured gatekeeper, suffering from bruises, was taken to University College Hospital in London.

8

In the world of big-money crime, art theft is only slightly less profitable than drug trafficking. It is estimated that almost £4 billion worth of art and antiques has been stolen in Britain in the last two years, but less than five per cent has been recovered.

Most works of art are stolen to order by wealthy collectors who move in respectable circles that are beyond the prying eyes of the police. Many stolen masterpieces are never seen by the public again. When, occasionally, gangs steal paintings for themselves, they do not attempt to sell them. Instead they usually demand a ransom for their return. But a stolen painting usually ends up with a tycoon who shows it only to close confidants.

(adapted from a report in *Today*)

1 The raid was carried out
a by a wealthy collector, who knew exactly what he wanted.
b by an art expert acting under orders.
c by an organized and violent gang of art thieves.
d by a professional thief.

2 The gatekeeper
a was beaten up outside the building.
b was forced to hand over his keys to the thief.
c was knocked unconscious before he could set off the alarm.
d was dragged inside the building after having his hands tied behind his back.

3 The thief
a is believed to have driven off in a red Ford Escort car at about half past five.
b is unlikely to be caught since there is little chance of recovering the paintings.
c is believed to have been working for someone who moves in respectable circles.
d is believed to have stolen the paintings for himself.

4 After the raid,
a the surrounding area was searched by the police.
b anyone who was hanging about in a suspicious manner was questioned by the police.
c the surrounding area was closed to traffic while the police made their enquiries.
d passers-by were taken to Holborn police station where they were questioned by detectives.

5 Most stolen paintings
a are usually sold by the thieves for a huge profit.
b are usually returned after a ransom has been paid.
c end up in private collections.
d are eventually seen by the public again.

8

Spotlight on vocabulary: crime and punishment

Answer each question. Then discuss the difference between the words or phrases in italics. Give examples.

1 Does a thief *rob* or *steal* money?
2 If you have been robbed, are you the *receiver* or *victim* of a crime?
3 If somebody has stolen money from you, have you been *robbed of your money* or *out of your money*?
4 If you see somebody doing something illegal, are you *witnessing* or *committing* a crime?
5 If it is thought that you have broken the law and you have to appear in court, does that mean you have been *convicted of a crime* or *charged with a crime*?
6 Is a minor crime – such as illegal parking – called an *offence* or *misbehaviour*?
7 In court, would you *swear at the judge* or *swear to tell the truth*?
8 Does a jury reach a *decision* or a *verdict*?
9 Are you *sent* or *sentenced* to a term in prison?
10 If you kill someone by accident, are you guilty of *murder* or *manslaughter*?
11 If you have two wives, are you guilty of *bigamy* or *forgery*?
12 In an English court, does the *judge* or the *defendant* wear a wig?
13 Do we say that someone is as *drunk* or *sober* as a judge?
14 Does a burglar *break into houses* or *mug people in the street*?
15 Do terrorists *hijack* or *kidnap* aeroplanes?
16 Are illegal drugs *hidden* or *smuggled* from country to country?
17 If a newspaper printed lies about you, would you *accuse* or *sue* the newspaper?
18 If you were found guilty of deliberately setting fire to a building, would you be convicted of *blackmail* or *arson*?
19 In England, has capital punishment been *abolished* or *banned*?
20 It is the job of lawyers to defend and prosecute people in court. Are these lawyers called *solicitors* or *barristers*?

Spotlight on phrasal verbs

Using *break* or *bring*, complete each sentence with a phrasal verb so that it means exactly the same as the sentence printed above it. You will need to use the following words: *about*, *down*, *off*, *out*, *round* and *up*.

The thief forced his way into the house.
The thief *broke into* the house.

1 He lost control of his emotions and cried like a child.
He … .

2 We have decided to end relations with our neighbouring countries.
We have decided to … .

3 The police dispersed the crowd of angry demonstrators.
The police … .

4 Our marriage ended because he drank too much.
Our marriage … .

5 The fire started on the second floor of the building.
The fire … .

6 I was raised by an aunt in Scotland.
I was … .

7 What has caused the sudden change in company policy?
What has … ?

8

8 Are there any other points you wish to raise?
Are there any other points you wish to ... ?

9 Throw some water on her face. That should make her regain consciousness.
Throw some water on her face. That should ... .

10 It was a difficult deal to negotiate but he managed to complete it successfully.
It was a difficult deal to negotiate but he managed to ... .

Exam tip

The following exercise tests grammatical precision, and you should get used to asking yourself the questions below.

- What type of word is required? An article, a negative, a noun, a pronoun, a verb, an adjective, an adverb, a conjunction or a preposition?
- What type of verb is required? Auxiliary, modal or main verb? Which tense? Gerund or infinitive? Present or past participle?
- Should the word be singular or plural?
- What type of pronoun is required? Subject, object, relative, possessive or reflexive?
- Does my answer sound right when I read the whole sentence? Does the whole sentence now follow on logically from the one before? Does the next sentence now follow on logically from the one I have just completed?

Spotlight on completion

Fill each of the numbered blanks in the following passage. Use only one word in each space.

Ali Baba and Cassim (1) ...brothers who lived in a town in Persia. Cassim was rich and famous, while Ali Baba was (2) ... poor (3) ... he had to (4) ... a living (5) ... cutting wood and selling it in the town.
One day when Ali Baba was in the forest he saw a number of horsemen coming (6) ... him, and fearing that they (7) ... be robbers he quickly (8) ... a tree and hid (9) ... .
There were forty horsemen (10) ... all, and when they came near the tree where Ali was (11) ..., they dismounted. After they (12) ... tied up their horses and fed them, they all turned and followed (13) ... leader to a nearby rock. 'Open Sesame,' cried the leader, and a door opened in the rock. The men entered one (14) ... one, and the leader followed. Then the door closed by itself.
Ali Baba waited, and after some time he saw the robbers filing out again. When they were out of (15) ..., he went (16) ... to the rock and called (17) ..., 'Open Sesame'. The door flew open at the words and Ali Baba stepped inside. He was (18) ... to find himself in a well-lit cavern, filled with all (19) ... of valuable goods piled one upon (20) ... .

Spotlight on spelling

Study the words for a minute. Then read out a word to a partner. Ask him or her to spell the word aloud. Check his or her spelling.

accuse	bruise	interrupting	solicitor
appreciate	demonstrator	mislaying	smuggled
architect	foreigners	negotiate	terrorist
barrister	guilty	offence	traditional
beauty	illegally	prosecute	undoubtedly

8

Pause for thought

What is the origin of the expression *to be caught red-handed*?

To be caught red-handed means to be caught in the act of crime. The guilt of the person is usually not in doubt. If you find a burglar in your living-room holding some valuables that belong to you, then that person is said *to have been caught red-handed.*

Red-handed means *hands red with blood.* The expression dates back to the time when it was almost impossible to prove that somebody was guilty of a crime unless the person confessed – usually under torture – or was caught in the act of committing a crime. One common crime was the killing of another man's cow, sheep or pig. There was also a law which forbade the killing of the king's deer in the forests of England. If a person was caught in possession of fresh meat, this was not usually enough to prove the person's guilt. It was only when a person was caught with both a dead animal and blood on his hands that there was enough evidence for the person to be arrested and then convicted.

Writing

Write an account of an exciting event or incident. End with the statement: *I shall not forget that day for as long as I live*. (120 – 180 words)

Speaking

1 Comment on this painting. Do you consider it a work of art? Would you call it a masterpiece?
2 If you had the money, would you be prepared to pay a million pounds for a painting by a famous artist?
3 Do you find abstract paintings interesting to look at? Do you consider abstract art to be 'real' art?
4 Do you think that art theft is a serious problem, or do you think that there are much more important things to worry about?
5 Have you visited an art gallery recently? Do you find art galleries boring? Do you think that admission to art galleries and museums should be free or do you think it is reasonable for them to charge a small entrance fee?

Unit 9

Accuracy building 1

Choose the most appropriate word or phrase to complete each statement. After deciding which is the correct answer, focus your attention on the alternatives. When can they be used?

1 Who are you going to … for in the next election?
a elect *b* vote *c* support *d* choose

2 The two cars were involved in a … collision.
a face to face *b* back to front *c* head-on *d* crash

3 A new set of stamps has been … by the Post Office to commemorate the Queen's birthday.
a issued *b* invented *c* published *d* stated

4 The story-line of a film or book is called the … .
a theme *b* cast *c* plot *d* history

5 I … my umbrella on the bus this morning.
a forgot *b* left *c* misplaced *d* abandoned

6 This new car has certain … that distinguish it from all the others on the market.
a characters *b* brands *c* features *d* models

7 Lawyers act on … of their clients.
a behalf *b* interest *c* representing *d* side

8 The money he inherited … him to start up his own business.
a entitled *b* ensured *c* enforced *d* enabled

9 She had to give up working on … of her ill health.
a owing *b* due *c* because *d* account

10 The roof is … again! When are you going to do something about it?
a collapsing *b* blown off *c* leaking *d* sinking

11 The wall needs another … of paint.
a layer *b* coat *c* cover *d* mixture

12 He … stealing the money.
a admitted *b* confessed *c* accepted *d* agreed

13 This cream should be thinly applied to the affected areas. If symptoms persist, … your doctor.
a examine *b* question *c* interrogate *d* consult

14 I'll … for you at eight o'clock.
a visit *b* pick up *c* call *d* collect

15 I don't think we should pick those apples yet. They don't look … .
a mature *b* prepared *c* ripe *d* green

16 I want you to learn these words by … .
a memory *b* heart *c* ear *d* word of mouth

17 The orchestra was … by Andre Previn.
a directed *b* composed *c* conducted *d* played

18 You'll find the travel agency … the end of the street.
a in *b* on *c* by *d* at

19 I work on the night … and don't get home till ten in the morning.
a spell *b* shift *c* rota *d* time

20 He's very good … his hands. He'll make an excellent craftsman.
a at *b* with *c* to *d* for

21 School fees must be paid in … . You cannot attend classes until you have paid for the course.
a time *b* advance *c* future *d* the future

22 I … for her straightaway. It was love at first sight.
a fell *b* was attracted *c* fell in love *d* was charmed

23 You ought to take a few days off. You look … out.
a weary *b* fatigued *c* exhausted *d* worn

24 A dog whistle is not … to the human ear.
a audible *b* visible *c* tangible *d* sensible

25 He's not modest at all. He's always blowing his own … .
a nose *b* wind *c* whistle *d* trumpet

Accuracy building 2

Now complete the following statements from memory. Do not look back at the previous exercise.

1 I shall certainly not … for that politician.
2 The two trains collided … .
3 A warrant has been … for his arrest.
4 The novel is well-written and has an exciting … .
5 Oh no! I've … the tickets at home.
6 She has the same striking … as her mother.
7 I am here on … of Thomas Green, who unfortunately cannot attend today's meeting.
8 The loan he obtained … him to set up his own company.
9 Please don't trouble yourself on my … .
10 One of the pipes is … . We'll have to call a plumber.
11 The door could do with a fresh … of paint.
12 She … stealing the money from the till.
13 You should … your doctor before going on a strict diet.
14 My boyfriend said he'd … for me at seven, but it's nine o'clock and he still hasn't turned up.
15 The pears are … and ready for picking.
16 I have to learn these phrases by … .
17 He has … some of the finest orchestras in the world.
18 Room ten is … the end of this corridor.
19 The night … begins at nine in the evening and finishes at five in the morning.
20 We need somebody practical; somebody who's good … his hands.
21 We have to book the tickets in … .
22 He was so attractive that she … for him straightaway.
23 It's been a tiring day. I'm really … out.
24 I was sitting too far away for his words to be … .
25 He never stops boasting. He's always blowing his own … .

9

Spotlight on offering, requesting and refusing

Finish each sentence in such a way that it means exactly the same as the sentence above it.

I shall not do it.
He refused *to do it*.

1 Shall I hoover the carpet for you?
Would you ... ?

2 Would you care for a brandy, Tony?
She offered ... .

3 Shall I do the shopping for you, Mum?
He offered ... .

4 You can borrow my lawn-mower if you like, Mr Smith.
I offered ... .

5 He offered me £500 for the furniture.
He made ... .

6 The offer was too good for him to refuse.
It was ... .

7 You couldn't possibly lend me £700, could you?
I don't ... ?

8 Please do not whistle. I am trying to concentrate.
Would you mind ... .

9 May I use your telephone?
Do you mind ... ?

10 Would it be all right for me to take a day off work next week?
Would you mind ... ?

11 Please don't leave me, Carol!
He begged ... .

12 'You can't watch television until you have done your homework!' she told Matthew.
She refused ... .

13 Nobody was surprised when he refused to co-operate.
His ... .

14 They did not let anybody enter the building until it had been thoroughly searched.
Nobody was ... .

15 He would not let me quote from his book.
He refused me ... .

9

Spotlight on question tags

Complete each statement with an appropriate question tag.

It's hot today, ... ?
It's hot today, *isn't it*?

1 He comes from Turkey, ... ?
2 She's gone to live abroad, ... ?
3 You didn't touch that, ... ?
4 She had to resign from her last job, ... ?
5 You haven't got a light, ... ?
6 You were here first, ... ?
7 You'd better hurry, ... ?
8 She'd like to see the photos, ... ?
9 That was kind of him, ... ?
10 He can swim, ... ?
11 There are a lot of people here tonight, ... ?
12 You will give it to her, ... ?
13 I am too old, ... ?
14 Let's try this restaurant, ... ?
15 Close the door, ... ?

Have a laugh

I stayed in a small village last summer. My landlady grew all her own vegetables and kept animals in her backyard.
On the first day one of her chickens died, so we had chicken casserole for dinner.
On the second day one of her pigs died, so we had pork chops for dinner.
On the third day one of her ducks died, so we had roast duck for dinner.
On the fourth day her husband died, so I left before dinner.

Reading

Read the passage below. Following the passage, you will find five unfinished statements. Decide which of the alternatives, *a*, *b*, *c* or *d*, best completes each statement.

KINDNESS TO ANIMALS

On World Day of Prayer for Animals next Thursday, the feast of St Francis of Assisi, animal-loving Roman Catholics will be celebrating a change in the attitude of their church towards animals. This year, Pope John Paul II said for the first time that 'animals possess a soul and that men must love and feel solidarity with our smaller brethren'.

For many years the church had taken the view that animals were without souls, an opinion taken from St Thomas Aquinas, the great Catholic theologian. Worse still, the idea of animals being without souls had sometimes been interpreted to mean that cruelty to them was not sinful.

Not so long ago an Italian archbishop claimed it was no sin to beat or starve a dog (because it had no soul) and in Britain a community of nuns saw nothing wrong in financing their religious life by running a battery-hen business, which was closed down for health reasons.

To persuade Catholics that kindness to animals is a moral requirement, the Catholic Study Circle for Animal Welfare has published a leaflet on the Pope's remarks.

The church's new attitude has the support of tradition. Animal-loving saints set a good example. One was St Kevin, a Celtic hermit, who is said to have been praying with an outstretched hand when a blackbird laid an egg in it. 'He remained neither closing nor withdrawing his hand ...until the young ones were fully hatched.' Another was St Martin of Porres, a Dominican, who persuaded the mice infesting his monastery to leave by giving them a shed in the garden where he fed them daily.

But the best model, of course, is St Francis of Assisi. He rescued hares in traps and put caught fish back into the lake. Not only did he preach to animals, but, says his biographer, Thomas of Celano, 'he would pick up worms from the road so that they should not be trodden underfoot by the passers-by'. Animals, we are told, responded to his love. One of his pet lambs would go to church and kneel down during the elevation of the host. And a pack of wolves, at his request, apparently changed their eating habits, abstaining from the flesh of men and farm animals.

This year's celebration of the saint's feast-day on October 4th will be particularly joyful for animal lovers. At last people can hope to meet much-loved pets in heaven!

(from an article in the *Daily Telegraph*)

1 Until recently,
a kindness to animals had been rare among Roman Catholics.
b the Roman Catholic church had taken the view that cruelty to animals was not sinful.
c animals had not possessed a soul.
d the Roman Catholic church had taken the view that not all living creatures possessed a soul.

2 We learn from the passage that
a some religious sisters in Britain stopped running a battery-hen business because of the Pope's remarks.
b an Italian archbishop used to beat and starve dogs.
c further information is available if you are interested in what the Pope said.
d animal-loving Catholics are going to have a feast on October 4th.

3 St Kevin is said to have
a been praying for a blackbird to lay an egg in his outstretched hand.
b let his hand be used as a nest.
c set a good example for animal-loving saints to follow.
d supported the church's new attitude towards animals.

4 We are told that
a St Francis of Assisi's pet lambs would go to church and kneel down during the elevation of the host.
b St Francis of Assisi persuaded a pack of wolves to stop eating meat.
c St Francis of Assisi would pick up worms from the road so that they would not get run over by passing vehicles.
d not only did St Francis of Assisi love animals, but he also spoke to them about God and other matters.

5 At last animal lovers
a can confidently expect to meet much-loved pets in heaven.
b will celebrate the feast of St Francis of Assisi in a joyful manner.
c can hope that there is life after death both for themselves and their pets.
d can officially celebrate the feast-day of St Francis of Assisi.

Spotlight on vocabulary: animals

Answer each question. Then discuss the difference between the words or phrases in italics. Give examples.

1 Is the meat from a sheep called *mutton* or *lamb*?
2 Is the meat from a deer called *beef* or *venison*?
3 Is the meat from a calf called *veal* or *pork*?
4 Are horses kept in a *stable* or a *kennel*?
5 Are young dogs called *kittens* or *puppies*?
6 Does a dog *bark* or *roar*?
7 Does a wolf *neigh* or *howl*?
8 If you reveal a secret, do you *take a rabbit out of a hat* or *let the cat out of the bag*?
9 Is the domestic cat a *wild* or *tame* animal?

10 Does a *bull* or a *donkey* have horns?
11 Does an elephant have a *trunk* or a *beak*?
12 Are you likely to see a flock of *goose* or *geese*?
13 What do farmers use to frighten birds from their fields, a *scarecrow* or a *hedgehog*?
14 If you have poor eyesight, are you as blind as *a bat* or *an owl*?
15 If you are feeling nervous, have you got *butterflies* or *worms* in your stomach?
16 If somebody threw a vase at you, would you *duck* or *leap like a frog?*
17 Would you expect to find a *herd of cattle* or a *flock of sheep* on a dairy farm?
18 Do snakes *crawl* or *gallop*?
19 Does a *squirrel* or a *bear* have a bushy tail?
20 Do some animals *migrate* or *emigrate* to warmer regions in winter?

Spotlight on phrasal verbs

Using *call, carry* or *catch*, complete each sentence with a phrasal verb so that it means exactly the same as the sentence printed above it. You will need to use the following words: *away, for, off, on, out, up* and *with*.

Could you ring me back in ten minutes?
Could you *call me back* in ten minutes?

1 The football match has been cancelled.
The football match has been … .

2 My brother has been summoned to do military service.
My brother has been … .

3 The job requires a certain amount of tact and discretion.
The job … .

4 He shouted to her to attract her attention.
He … .

5 The vicar said he would pay them a visit.
The vicar said he would … .

6 He has had to go somewhere on business. I'm afraid he won't be back until the day after tomorrow.
He has been … .

7 Please continue with your work.
Please … .

8 A soldier is punished if he does not obey an order.
A soldier is punished if he does not … .

9 I don't think that style of dress will become popular.
I don't think that style of dress will … .

10 He is too far ahead. I'll never draw level with him.
He is too far ahead. I'll never … .

Pause for thought

What is meant by the term *a white elephant*?

We use the expression to describe a gift that causes more trouble or cost than it is worth. An expensive item that turns out to be useless is known as *a white elephant.*

The term is derived from an old-time custom of the Kings of Siam who used to give a white elephant to any courtier who annoyed them. The animals were regarded as sacred, but their upkeep was so costly that anyone who received one was apt to be financially ruined.

Spotlight on completion

Fill each of the numbered blanks in the following passage. Use only one word in each space.

Last Tuesday I went to the bank as (1) … and afterwards did some (2) … for my wife. I never (3) … her drive my new car in town because two years ago she (4) … an accident in the High Street.
(5) … coming out of the butcher's, I (6) … to my horror that my little grey Citroen (7) … disappeared. (8) … I could not see a policeman near the shops, I went at (9) … to the police station. There I saw a young inspector who (10) … to live in the (11) … neighbourhood as myself.
'Good morning, Peter,' I said, (12) … his hand. '(13) … pleased I am to see an old friend!' The inspector looked at me (14) … saying a word. 'Well,' I continued, a (15) … surprised, 'I hope you aren't (16) … to ask me (17) … my name and address!'
He then slowly took a pencil (18) … of his pocket and replied: 'You (19) … find your car in the yard behind this building. You know very well it is (20) … to park opposite the town hall.'

Exam tip

- Careless handwriting will lose you marks.
- Every word you write down in the exam will be looked at carefully by an examiner. If there is the slightest doubt about the spelling of a word, it will be counted as a mistake. One wrong letter means that the whole word is wrong. If an examiner has any difficulty in distinguishing one letter from another, he will simply regard it as a mistake on your part.
- The letters *a, e, h, i, j, r, l* and *t* are often written in such a careless way that an examiner has no alternative but to penalise the candidate – even though the word may have been correctly spelt. Make sure that you do not lose marks because of your handwriting!
- If you make a mistake, put one line through the word and write your correction above it. It is best not to use correcting fluid (such as Tipp-Ex) in the exam. You will simply waste time waiting for the fluid to dry. More importantly, it quite often happens that a student using Tipp-Ex forgets to write in the correction afterwards, thus leaving blanks which may cost quite a few marks.

Spotlight on spelling

Study the words for a minute. Then read out a word to a partner. Ask him or her to spell the word aloud. Check his or her spelling.

butcher's	orchestra
cancelled	particularly
cattle	persuade
collision	possess
distinguish	recipient
furniture	religious
inherited	requires
kneel	summoned
offered	thoroughly
opposite	vehicle

9

Writing

It was four o'clock in the morning and I was fast asleep. Suddenly I was awoken by a loud noise. Somebody was knocking furiously on my front door. Continue the story. (120 –180 words)

Speaking

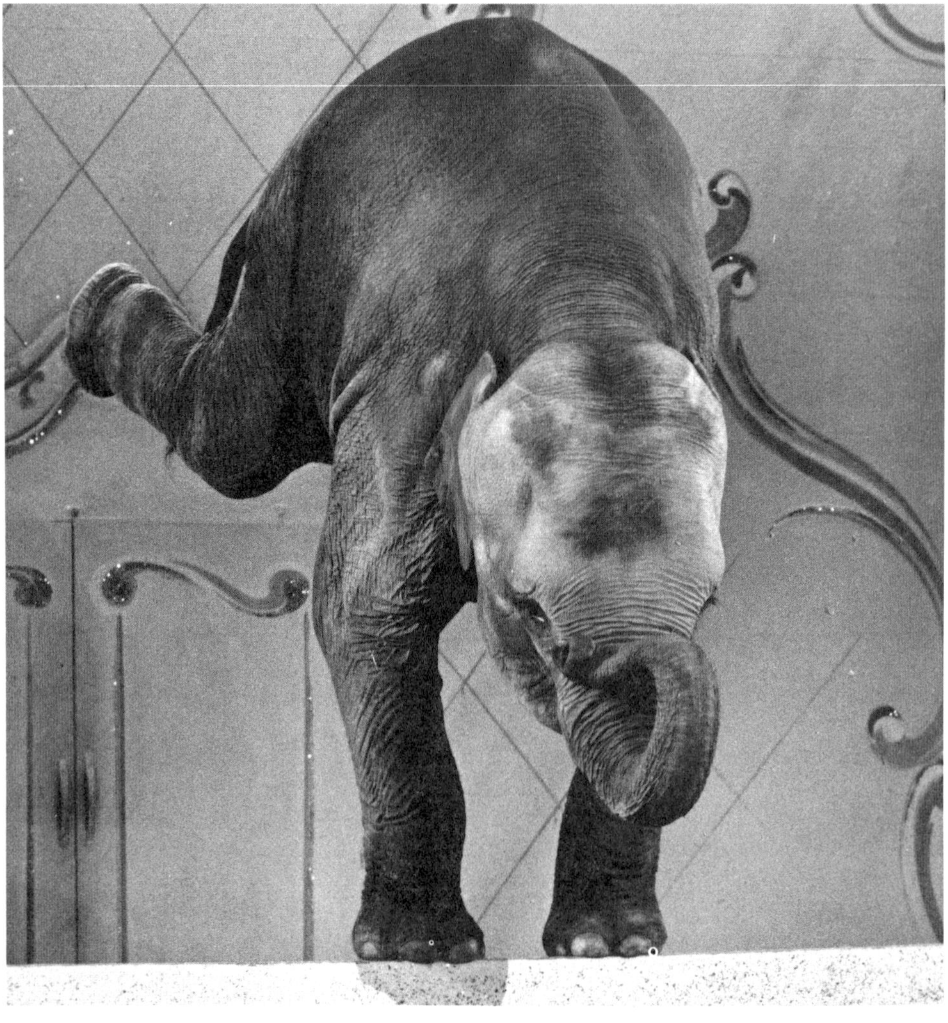

1 Does this photograph make you smile or make you angry? Do you feel sorry for the elephant or do you admire the elephant for its ability to perform circus tricks?
2 Is it wrong to train animals to perform circus tricks?
3 Do you think it is cruel to keep wild animals in zoos? Should we get rid of zoos?
4 Do you think circus animals lead a more interesting and active life than animals in zoos?
5 Do you think it is right to keep animals as pets?

Unit 10

Accuracy building 1

Choose the most appropriate word or phrase to complete each statement. After deciding which is the correct answer, focus your attention on the alternatives. When can they be used?

1 I'm sorry I'm late. I was … up by the traffic.
a delayed *b* congested *c* blocked *d* held

2 He … into her eyes and told her that she was the most beautiful woman in the world.
a glimpsed *b* glanced *c* gazed *d* stared

3 The orchestra will have a final … this afternoon before tonight's concert.
a training *b* practise *c* rehearsal *d* repeat

4 Is there a car … near here?
a park *b* space *c* parking *d* meter

5 She was … the point of leaving when the phone rang.
a about *b* on *c* to *d* from

6 He did not … tell her the truth.
a want *b* dare *c* risk *d* wish

7 I've been lifting heavy objects all morning and my back … .
a pains *b* stretches *c* aches *d* strains

8 She is … of what she did.
a ashamed *b* shameful *c* shame *d* shameless

9 He looks really embarrassed. He's … as red as a beetroot.
a painted *b* gone *c* coloured *d* blush

10 He's lost most of his hair. He's almost completely … .
a shaven *b* naked *c* bare *d* bald

11 They have … a campaign against the dumping of nuclear waste in the North Sea.
a fight *b* began *c* embarked *d* launched

12 Sheila is … to do well in the exam. That's why she's studying so hard.
a determined *b* decided *c* chosen *d* resolving

13 There are chestnut trees on … side of the path.
a both *b* double *c* other *d* either

14 The demonstrators … past the town hall.
a gathered *b* protested *c* marched *d* manifested

15 All my plans have fallen … . I shall not be working abroad after all.
a through *b* off *c* over *d* down

16 She blamed me … what happened.
a to *b* on *c* why *d* for

17 'Darling,' he … in her ear, 'will you marry me?'
a shouted *b* yelled *c* shrieked *d* whispered

18 Nobody's going to buy that rubbish. It's … .
a worthless *b* invaluable *c* unworthy *d* priceless

10

19 Body temperature is ... with a thermometer.
a judged *b* calculated *c* measured *d* estimated

20 A hen sits on her eggs until they ... .
a hatch *b* poach *c* scramble *d* boil

21 What's it called? Wait a moment, it's on the ... of my tongue.
a edge *b* point *c* tip *d* peak

22 I'd have helped you if you ... me.
a would have asked *b* would ask *c* had asked *d* asked

23 Go down the hill ... the church and then turn left.
a until *b* as far as *c* nearby *d* till

24 Hot curries don't agree ... me.
a to *b* with *c* on *d* for

25 Let's wait until the weather clears ... .
a up *b* off *c* better *d* improvement

Accuracy building 2

Now complete the following statements from memory. Do not look back at the previous exercise.

1 He phoned to say that he has been ... up and will be arriving late.
2 He ... at the stars in the sky.
3 The final ... of the play will take place on Wednesday.
4 We drove around the town looking for a car ... .
5 There were many times when I was ... the point of giving up.
6 He did not ... tell his father that he had failed the exam.
7 I've been digging in the garden and my back ... .
8 That was not a nice thing to do. You should be ... of yourself.
9 She's ... as red as a beetroot.
10 Many men grow ... as they get older.
11 The new ship will be ... next month.
12 I am ... to do better next time.
13 There are rose bushes on ... side of the garden path.
14 The demonstrators ... past the Embassy.
15 The project has fallen ... .
16 They blamed me ... the accident.
17 'Could you pass me a tissue?' he ... to his wife in the theatre.
18 I'm afraid these items are ... . You have wasted your money.
19 The boy ... the length of the table with his ruler.
20 We don't know how many of the eggs will ... .
21 I'm trying to remember. It's on the ... of my tongue.
22 If you ... me, I would have told you what to do.
23 You should go ... the traffic lights and then turn right.
24 Fried bread doesn't agree ... me.
25 The weather is clearing ... at last.

10

Spotlight on conjunctions

Finish each of the following sentences in such a way that it means exactly the same as the sentence printed above it.

It was because of him that we all survived.
It was thanks *to him that we all survived.*

1 Despite being rich, he is not happy.
Although … .

2 Although he lacks experience, I still think he should be promoted.
Despite his … .

3 Despite being severely handicapped, he is always cheerful and full of life.
Despite the … .

4 Although he has a very quick temper, he is a very good manager.
In spite … .

5 He made a huge loss last year, but he still refuses to sell his company.
He refuses to sell his company even … .

6 I don't care if they offer me £10 million, I shall still not sell the painting.
Even … .

7 I'll inform you the moment I have any news.
I'll inform you as … .

8 When she arrived home, she discovered that she had left her keys at the office.
On … .

9 I was leaving when the postman arrived.
Just … .

10 I will only go if you accompany me.
I will go as … .

11 Besides playing the piano, he plays three other instruments.
Not only … .

12 I set off early in order to avoid any heavy traffic on the roads.
I set off early so … .

13 It seems that you have made a very big mistake.
It looks … .

14 There is ice on the runways. That's why the airport is closed.
The airport is closed … .

15 He was awarded a medal in recognition of his bravery.
He was awarded a medal because he … .

10

Spotlight on *(be/get) used to*

Finish each sentence in such a way that it means exactly the same as the sentence above it. Use *used to*, *be used to*, or *get used to*.

You'll soon get accustomed to the climate.
You'll soon *get used to* the climate.

1 She played tennis at least twice a week when she was younger.
She … .

2 You will soon get into the habit of getting up early.
You … .

3 This is the first time I have worked in a restaurant.
I … .

4 When I lived in the country, I would go for long walks every day.
When I lived in the country, I … .

5 I have often driven an automatic car.
I … .

6 She is no longer my best friend.
She … .

7 There was once a church at the corner, but it was pulled down a few years ago.
There … .

8 I hardly ever stay up late.
I … .

9 He wasn't so mean before.
He … .

10 He has not lived on his own before.
He … .

Have a laugh

Two men were climbing a particularly difficult mountain when one of them suddenly fell down a crevice 500 feet deep.
'Are you all right, Tom?' shouted the man at the top of the crevice.
'I'm still alive, thank goodness, Fred,' came the reply.
'Here grab this rope,' said Fred, throwing a rope down to Tom.
'I can't grab it,' shouted Tom. 'My arms are broken.'
'Well, fit it around your legs.'
'I'm afraid I can't do that either,' apologised Tom. 'My legs are broken.'
'Put the rope in your mouth,' shouted Fred.
So Tom put the rope in his mouth and Fred began to pull him up to safety. 490 feet … 400 feet … 300 feet … 200 feet … 100 feet … 50 feet … and then Fred called: 'Are you all right, Tom?'
'Yeeeeeeeee…

Reading

Read the passage below. Following the passage, you will find five unfinished statements. Decide which of the alternatives, *a*, *b*, *c* or *d*, best completes each statement.

APPROPRIATE DRESS

The thermometer hit 95°F. The deputy chief accountant came in wearing shorts. The chief accountant hit the roof. 'What shall I do?' he asked the personnel director. 'Send him home,' was the instant reply. 'He is asking for a confrontation and you cannot back off without losing your grip on discipline.'

The accountant was sent home to change. Such is the power of the grapevine that, within minutes, the personnel director had to deny a factory floor rumour that a director had been sacked for wearing a T-shirt to a board meeting.

That incident took place at a northern engineering firm of traditional values, at the height of last week's heatwave, amid reports of policemen in Bournemouth being sent out on patrol in Bermuda shorts and overheated lawyers being allowed to remove wig and gown in court.

10

Increasingly, as dress becomes more and more casual at home, in the pub and in the street, office workers are challenging the tyranny of collar, tie and sober suit.

When temperatures soar, a manager with any compassion will see justice in demands for relaxing the dress code. Usually, nothing will be said. Ties will be loosened and jackets removed, revealing short-sleeved shirts, without comment. Shorts, T-shirts and sandals are, however, another matter.

The heat hits men hardest. Convention has little to say about women's office clothing, which allows far greater choice. Summer frocks are perfectly acceptable in the average office provided the neckline does not plunge too far.

Management's main fear is that visitors from headquarters, clients or suppliers will turn up unexpectedly to see key staff. If they come into the conference room dressed for the beach, the meeting may get off on the wrong foot.

'You need to consider what impression you are making on customers,' says Brian Lilley, director general of the Institute of Personnel Management. 'It can work the opposite way. If you are heavily overdressed and sweltering in a three-piece suit, they might not come away with a good impression of your business efficiency.'

(from an article in the *Daily Telegraph*)

1 When the deputy chief accountant came to work improperly dressed, the chief accountant
a handled the situation with tact and diplomacy.
b took instant, but discreet, action.
c flew into a rage.
d lost his temper and dismissed him after consulting the personnel director.

2 The deputy chief accountant was sent home
a for not being conventionally dressed
b for wearing a T-shirt to a board meeting.
c for conforming to traditional standards of dress.
d for not wearing shorts to work.

3 During a heatwave, a manager with any compassion will usually
a demand that the dress code be relaxed.
b allow shorts, T-shirts and sandals to be worn.
c be less strict in his attitude to dress.
d say nothing if staff wear casual dress.

4 According to the passage,
a there are no rules governing women's office clothing.
b women have a slightly greater choice in what they can wear to work.
c women are not affected by the heat.
d rules governing women's clothes are generally more flexible.

5 Insistence on formal dress at all times
a is a sign of business efficiency.
b always impresses customers.
c may not always produce the desired effect.
d is based on management's fear that visitors, clients or suppliers from headquarters might turn up unexpectedly to see key staff.

10

Spotlight on vocabulary: dress

Answer each question. Then discuss the difference between the words or phrases in italics. Give examples.

1 Does a tailor make a suit from *cloth* or *clothing*?
2 If you have a silk tie, has the tie been *knitted* or *woven* from silk?
3 To sew on a button, would you use *a needle and thread* or *a safety-pin and cotton*?
4 Before taking off your shoes, would you *untie* or *do up* your shoe-laces?
5 If you wish to buy a blouse to go with your blue skirt, do you want a blouse that will *suit* or *match* your skirt?
6 Would a man normally buy a pair of *stockings* or *gloves* for himself?
7 Is a vest usually worn *under* or *over* a shirt?
8 Is a dressing-gown usually worn *inside* or *outside* the house?
9 Does a mechanic wear *overalls* or an *apron*?
10 Would you use a *strap* or a *belt* to hold up your trousers?
11 If your trousers are baggy, are they very *loose* or too *tight*?
12 Is a tramp usually dressed in *smart* or *shabby* clothes?
13 Who is more likely to be dressed in rags, a *beggar* or a *king*?
14 Is a bracelet worn around the *wrist* or the *waist*?
15 On a special occasion, would a woman wear a *bow-tie* or a *necklace*?
16 To shorten a garment, do you *take it in* or *take it up*?
17 In a shop, would you *try on* or *try out* a dress?
18 If you are dressed, have you *got your clothes on* or are you *putting your clothes on*?
19 Before taking off a shirt, would you *unbutton* or *undo* the buttons?
20 Before going out on a cold wintry day, would you *wrap yourself up well* or *wear out your warmest clothes*?

Exam tip

- Treat phrasal verbs as friends not enemies! They form an essential part of the English language and their purpose is to help you to express yourself precisely and concisely.
- Always learn a phrasal verb in its proper context. That is to say, learn to recognise phrasal verbs in sentences and learn these sentences as a whole. There is little point in learning a list of phrasal verbs with their definitions if you are not going to remember how they are actually used.
- Keep phrasal verbs in perspective. The exam does not consist of hundreds of phrasal verbs! Be selective. Do not try to learn by heart every phrasal verb you come across.

Spotlight on phrasal verbs

Using *come*, complete each sentence with a phrasal verb so that it means exactly the same as the sentence printed above it. You will need to use the following words: *across*, *against*, *down*, *into*, *on*, *out*, *round*, *up* and *with*.

The bill amounted to £40.
The bill *came to* £40.

1 She regained consciousness a few minutes ago.
She … .

2 She has inherited a fortune.
She … .

3 A problem has arisen regarding the new contract.
A problem … .

4 We didn't expect to be faced with such a problem.
We didn't expect to … .

5 The new magazine is being issued tomorrow.
The new magazine … .

6 I discovered it quite by chance as I was clearing out the attic.
I … .

7 Nobody has thought of a solution to the problem
Nobody … .

8 Hurry up or we'll be late!
… !

9 During a sale, prices are reduced.
During a sale, prices … .

10 Why don't you pay us a visit one evening next week?
Why don't you … ?

Pause for thought

What is a *sweater* and how did it get its name?

A *sweater* is a thick woollen jersey or jumper.

Horse-racing was as popular in the nineteenth century as it is today, and the training of race horses was taken very seriously. During training sessions, a horse would wear a special blanket that made it sweat freely. Obviously, there was but one logical name for it.

Later, it became fashionable for athletes and other sportsmen to work off excessive weight by wearing heavy flannel underwear during training sessions. Naturally, these were also called *sweaters*.

About 1940, the fashion industry started to produce woollen *sweaters*. Promoted as both casual and glamorous wear (worn by film stars in sports cars and by officers in the navy and air force), the *sweater* soon became fashionable.

Spotlight on completion

Fill each of the numbered blanks in the following passage. Use only one word in each space.

In one of the large (1) … of China there once lived a tailor, (2)… name was Mustapha. Mustapha was very poor, and he found (3) … hard to provide food (4) … himself, his wife, and his (5) … child, Aladdin. Aladdin was a very naughty and lazy boy. He (6) … never do (7) … his parents wished (8) … to do, but played in the streets from morning till night with boys (9) … were as naughty as himself.

When Aladdin was old (10) … to learn a trade, his father took him into his (11) … shop and began to show him (12) … he should use the needle. It was a complete (13) … of time. Aladdin had had his way for so long now that he could not settle (14) … to work. His father (15) … many hours trying to (16) … him to change his ways, but Aladdin took no (17) … of anything he said. Worn out, Mustapha became ill and died shortly afterwards.

The poor widow thought that her son would now (18) … an effort to earn a little money, but Aladdin was as idle as ever. In despair, the good woman sold all the things (19) … the shop, and with the money and a little she could earn by spinning she managed to get (20) … .

10

Spotlight on spelling

Study the words for a minute. Then read out a word to a partner. Ask him or her to spell the word aloud. Check his or her spelling.

accustomed	compassion	nineteenth	theatre
appropriate	discipline	personnel	thermometer
bracelet	embarrassed	rehearsal	through
campaign	knitted	severely	unexpectedly
casual	naughty	shrieked	woollen

Writing

I was walking along a quiet country lane with a friend of mine when suddenly … Continue the story. (120 – 180 words)

Spotlight on pronunciation

Pay particular attention to any word ending in *-ed* in the following sentences.

1 We had arranged to meet at six, but he arrived at eight.
2 I asked her a question and she answered it correctly.
3 Although he was embarrassed, he continued with the speech.
4 He informed her that he had changed his mind.
5 The box contained one hundred pencils.
6 They discussed it at length and eventually reached a decision.
7 The room was fully furnished and beautifully decorated.
8 She waited for a moment and then knocked again, but nobody opened the door.
9 The police examined all the evidence and decided that they had arrested the wrong man.
10 I hoped he would be encouraged by the news.
11 I'm interested in antiques.
12 She introduced me to her friends and suggested we had dinner together.
13 She looked at the letter for a few seconds and then nodded.
14 She laughed but he managed to keep a straight face.
15 The speech lasted too long and nobody was amused.
16 She packed her bags and walked out on me.
17 I had promised her something special, so I picked the most expensive ring on display.
18 He returned the money he had borrowed from me.
19 She was really annoyed because I hadn't remembered to post the letter even though she had reminded me the evening before.
20 I shared a flat with two friends but we soon started to quarrel, so I moved to another flat.
21 He studied hard and passed the exam.
22 They were rescued from the mountain and transported to hospital by helicopter.
23 He used to live in London.
24 He used his handkerchief to stop the bleeding.
25 I switched on the television and watched the football match.

Unit 11

Accuracy building 1

Choose the most appropriate word or phrase to complete each statement. After deciding which is the correct answer, focus your attention on the alternatives. When can they be used?

1 There is a hole … one of my socks.
a on *b* in *c* over *d* below

2 He is … blame. It was his fault.
a for *b* at *c* to *d* with

3 He gave the dog a friendly … on the head.
a thump *b* blow *c* pat *d* hug

4 I'm afraid it is not as simple as that. What we have seen is just the tip of the … .
a mountain *b* iceberg *c* finger *d* rubbish

5 The hotel is set high on a cliff with a breathtaking … of the bay below.
a sight *b* view *c* look *d* vision

6 There's a … in here. Would you mind closing the door?
a current *b* drought *c* gust of wind *d* draught

7 I don't … your position at all. I'm glad I'm not in your shoes.
a envy *b* wish *c* jealous of *d* seek

8 Excuse me. Could you … me to the nearest tube station, please?
a guide *b* show *c* tell *d* direct

9 The flash of lightning in the dark sky was followed by a loud … of thunder.
a explosion *b* clap *c* murmur *d* rattle

10 Children love reading or listening to fairy … .
a stories *b* jokes *c* legends *d* tales

11 He is married … a woman half his age.
a to *b* with *c* by *d* for

12 What was the reason? I'd like to know why … .
a did you do it *b* you did it *c* was it done *d* had you done it

13 They're no longer friends. They've … out with each other.
a split *b* separated *c* argued *d* fallen

14 Excuse me, but I couldn't help … your conversation. I think I might be able to help you.
a eavesdropping *b* spying on *c* observing *d* overhearing

15 I can't find my swimming … .
a briefs *b* pants *c* trunks *d* trousers

16 I'm feeling a bit … . I think I'll have a couple of biscuits.
a starving *b* famished *c* empty *d* peckish

17 'Too many cooks spoil the broth' is an English … .
a idiom *b* colloquialism *c* proverb *d* simile

18 I'm just going to … this orange.
a skin *b* uncover *c* undo *d* peel

19 You should keep clear of the boss this morning. He's in a really foul ... .
a temperament *b* mood *c* ill-temper *d* grumpy

20 She ... with astonishment when she saw who it was.
a uttered *b* gasped *c* burst *d* shivered

21 The village priest is a wise man. Everybody ... him.
a respect *b* obeys *c* listen to *d* looks up to

22 Many people use face-cream to try and prevent their skin from becoming ... .
a wrinkled *b* corrugated *c* creased *d* crumpled

23 You ought to mind your own business and not ... your nose where it does not belong!
a push *b* pull *c* prod *d* poke

24 The child knelt down and ... a prayer before getting into bed.
a explained *b* told *c* said *d* spoke

25 I've never been on good ... with my neighbours. We simply don't get on.
a relation *b* rapport *c* terms *d* relationship

Accuracy building 2

Now complete the following statements from memory. Do not look back at the previous exercise.

1 Don't put on that shirt. It's got a hole ... it.
2 I admit that I'm ... blame. It was my fault.
3 'Well done!' she said, giving him a ... on the back.
4 That's just the tip of the ... .
5 The ... from the top of the hill is really marvellous.
6 Would you mind closing the window? I can feel a ... in here.
7 I don't ... him. He's in a very difficult position.
8 Could you ... me to the nearest post office, please?
9 The ... of thunder was so loud that it woke us up.
10 The Grimm brothers wrote some very famous fairy ... .
11 I'm sure you've met her before. She's married ... Michael Brown's brother.
12 Tell me why ... . I would really like to know.
13 I've ... out with my girlfriend.
14 ... is by accident, whereas eavesdropping is by design.
15 I need to buy a pair of swimming ... .
16 If you are feeling ... , there's a bag of crisps on the kitchen table.
17 A ... is a traditional saying.
18 Who is going to ... the potatoes?
19 I wouldn't see her just yet if I were you. She's in a very bad ... .
20 She ... with astonished delight when she unwrapped her present.
21 Mr Smith is a highly respected teacher. Everybody in the school ... him.
22 The farmer's skin had become deeply tanned and ... from too much exposure to the sun.
23 Please do not ... your nose into matters that do not concern you!
24 On her way to work, she popped into a church and ... a quick prayer for her husband who was seriously ill.
25 He is still on good ... with his ex-wife. They are no longer married, but they remain good friends.

11

Spotlight on the gerund or infinitive (1)

Finish each sentence in such a way that it means exactly the same as the sentence above it.

He managed to do it. He succeeded *in doing it.*

1 I remember that film. I saw it two years ago.
I remember ... .

2 He did not forget to send her a birthday card.
He remembered ... .

3 As far as I can recall, I didn't mention it to anyone.
I don't remember ... .

4 An attempt was made on the President's life.
Someone tried ... .

5 Let's see what happens if you press the red button.
Try ... .

6 She made an effort to smile even though she was in great pain.
She tried ... .

7 Why don't you adjust the aerial?
Try ... .

8 I wish you wouldn't make so much noise.
Please stop ... .

9 He stopped because he wanted to check the brakes.
He stopped ... .

10 They don't serve lunch after three o'clock.
They stop ... .

11 Thank you for writing to me. It was very nice of you.
It was very nice ... .

12 You shouldn't have criticized her in front of the others.
It was wrong ... .

13 You needn't have gone to so much trouble.
It wasn't necessary ... .

14 I didn't do it on purpose.
I didn't mean ... .

15 If I accept the job, I will lose my place at university.
If I accept the job, it will mean ... .

16 I will earn more money in my new job, but I will have to work longer hours.
I will earn more money in my new job, but it will mean ... .

17 With Tony's help, I decorated my flat.
Tony helped ... .

18 He was unable to refrain from laughing.
He couldn't help ... .

19 With the help of the tablets, I got over my depression.
The tablets helped ... .

20 I feel sorry for her. I can't help it.
I can't help ... .

11

Reading

Read the passage below. Following the passage, you will find five unfinished statements. Decide which of the alternatives, *a*, *b*, *c* or *d*, best completes each statement.

STRANGER THAN FICTION

Even people who believe in ghosts might find it just a little difficult to accept the idea of a haunted bingo hall! But the Top Rank bingo hall in Morden, Surrey, is just that, according to some stories.

The building opened in 1937 as a cinema and was converted into a bingo hall in the early sixties. Before that, though, there had been three deaths. A nightwatchman was found dead, a builder fell to his death while the building was being converted and a third worker fell down a flight of stairs.

There's nothing mysterious about that - after all, people die all the time. What are harder to explain are the complaints from local residents about the noise of the cinema's organ being played late at night - years after the instrument had been removed.

There have also been many sightings of a mysterious apparition in grey who is believed to be the ghost of the dead builder. The staff have even given him a name, according to Mr Thomas, the manager. He's called Fred!

A ghost in a bingo hall might seem a bit odd, but what about a ghost bus? For years a ghost bus in London was blamed for causing accidents hours after normal buses had stopped running. At least one fatal accident was caused by cars swerving to avoid it. Later, the junction at which the bus was most frequently sighted was altered and the bus was never seen again.

Haunted bingo halls and ghost buses might sound a bit improbable, but is a ghost in a medieval castle any more likely?

The Hermitage Castle in Roxburghshire, Scotland dates back to the fourteenth century. At one time the castle belonged to Lord Soulis, who is said to have murdered children from nearby farms in cruel and horrific ways. Eventually, the locals stormed the castle, bound its owner in a 'blanket' of lead and boiled him alive. Ever since, there have been reports of horrible screams from the castle...

So does all this mean that ghosts are real? One group which would like to find out is the Association for the Scientific Study of Anomalous Phenomena, a registered charity run by volunteers. We spoke to Dr Hugh Pincott from ASSAP about what the Association does.

'We're there to investigate. We deal with 'traditional' phenomena like ghosts, poltergeists, UFOs and so on, as well as more modern areas like crop circles.'

One of the problems, according to Dr Pincott, is eliminating normal explanations.

'There was a case in South London where the occupants of a flat were complaining of a mysterious smell. In the end, it turned out to be an immersion heater short-circuiting! The bakelite in the switch was decomposing, causing the smell and eventually burning out the whole heater!

Roughly two thirds to three quarters of the cases we investigate turn out to have perfectly natural explanations - but the rest are harder to explain.'

(from an article in *Prime Time*)

11

1 According to the passage, the Top Rank bingo hall in Morden
a was the scene of three mysterious deaths.
b might seem a very unlikely place for a ghost to haunt.
c is said to be haunted by the ghosts of three people who died in the building.
d has an organ inside which is played late at night, much to the annoyance of local residents.

2 The building in Morden
a was converted into a bingo hall around 1965.
b is said to be haunted by a ghost called Fred, who fell down a flight of stairs while the building was being converted.
c is associated with two separate mysteries.
d is now owned by a man called Thomas, whose staff are so convinced that a ghost really exists that they have even given him a name.

3 Lord Soulis
a owned the Hermitage Castle some time in the fourteenth century.
b was killed in a horrible manner and then his body was immersed in boiling water.
c met a horrible death at the hands of the local people.
d was the owner of a castle in England and is said to have murdered local children in particularly cruel ways.

4 The Association for the Scientific Study of Anomalous Phenomena
a is a group which believes ghosts are real.
b is a group which believes that phenomena like ghosts and poltergeists have perfectly natural explanations.
c is an association of scientists who are paid to investigate unusual events and abnormal occurrences.
d is a non-profit-making organization which looks into reports of such phenomena as ghosts and UFOs.

5 According to Dr Pincott, a mysterious smell in a South London flat
a turned out to be the result of an electrical fault.
b turned out to be a trick.
c turned out to have a perfectly natural explanation, just like a third to a quarter of all cases investigated.
d turned out to be a decomposing immersion heater.

Spotlight on adjectives ending in *-ing* or *-ed*

Complete each statement by forming an appropriate adjective from the verb given in the right-hand column. Each adjective should end in *-ed* or *-ing*.

1	I felt completely … .	exhaust
2	Would you like to hear an … story?	amuse
3	Her exam results were extremely … .	disappoint
4	He's an … person to talk to.	interest
5	I was … when I heard the news.	shock
6	It was a … race from start to finish.	thrill
7	The police are … by his disappearance.	puzzle
8	I am … about her.	worry
9	I find his attitude very … .	annoy
10	It was a … experience.	terrify
11	It's a … habit.	disgust
12	He looks very … with himself.	please
13	Cricket can be a very … game.	excite

14	It's a ... book.	fascinate
15	I'm ... . I've got nothing to do.	bore
16	I am ... at you.	surprise
17	I find this exercise rather	confuse
18	He was ... by the work she had done.	impress
19	It was an ... situation.	embarrass
20	It was a long and ... journey.	tire

Have a laugh

Three men were on a fishing trip. Their boat was wrecked in a storm, but they managed to swim to a deserted island.
For the first few days everything went well. But after a week, two of the three men became quite depressed. One of them, a farmer, missed his farm and family. The other longed for his native city, where he was a taxi-driver. The third man, a happy-go-lucky type, was enjoying himself; finding the experience rather peaceful and very interesting.
One day, as the farmer walked along the beach with the others, he came across an ancient lamp. And when he rubbed it, a genie appeared.
'Because you have freed me from my prison,' said the genie, 'I shall grant each of you one wish.'
'I'd like to be back on my farm,' the farmer said.
Puff! He disappeared.
'I wish I was driving my taxi again,' the taxi-driver said.
Puff! He disappeared too.
'And what is your wish?' the genie asked the third man.
'Gosh,' he said, 'I'm rather lonely without the other two here. I wish they were back here with me.'
Puff! Puff!

Spotlight on vocabulary: fact and fiction

Answer each question. Then discuss the difference between the words or phrases in italics. Give examples.

1 You are in a desert and an oasis suddenly appears before your eyes. You approach the oasis and it disappears. Was the oasis a *mirage* or a *miracle*?
2 If you saw a ghost, would you be *frightened* or *frightening*?
3 If somebody has a powerful imagination, is that person *imaginary* or *imaginative*?
4 If you have a lively imagination, have you got a *vivid* or a *creative* imagination?
5 If a story has been invented, has it been *made up* or *made out*?
6 If you do not tell lies, are you a *true* or *truthful* person?
7 Does a newspaper *state* or *narrate* facts?
8 Is a novel *a work of fiction* or *a factual account of somebody's life*?
9 Is a nightmare a type of *dream* or *illusion*?
10 Does a magician perform *tricks* or *spells*?
11 If you have been fooled by somebody, have you been *taken in* or *taken over*?
12 If an advertisement deliberately causes the public to gain the wrong impression of a product because the facts have not been properly stated, is the advertisement *misinformed* or *misleading*?
13 Is a tall story one that is *difficult to believe* or one that *takes a long time to read*?

14 Is Sherlock Holmes a *character in a book* or a *characteristic of a book*?
15 If you face facts, are you a *realist* or a *realistic*?
16 If you have your head in the clouds, are you a *day-dreamer* or a *sleep-walker*?
17 If a story is unbelievable, is it an *incredible* or *credulous* story?
18 If something is impossible to believe, is it *past* or *beyond* belief?
19 If you are looking at something in total disbelief, does that mean you can hardly believe your *instincts* or *eyes*?
20 Do the letters UFO stand for *'unknown foreign object'* or *'unidentified flying object'*?

Spotlight on phrasal verbs

Using *cut, draw* or *do*, complete each sentence with a phrasal verb so that it means exactly the same as the sentence printed above it. You will need to use the following words: *away, down, off, on, out, up, with* and *without*.

He interrupted our conversation.
He *cut in on* our conversation.

1 Why did you cut it into pieces?
Why ... ?

2 He was advised to reduce the amount of meat he ate.
He was advised to ... .

3 The water rose higher and higher and I suddenly found myself separated from the rest of the group.
The water rose higher and higher and I suddenly found myself ... .

4 The van stopped outside the cinema and two men jumped out.
The van ... .

5 I'll withdraw some money from the bank this afternoon.
I'll ... .

6 Make sure that the contract is prepared by a good lawyer.
Make sure that the contract ... .

7 The kitchen walls need a fresh coat of paint.
The kitchen walls could ... .

8 When did you decorate the kitchen? It looks really smart.
When ... .

9 They ought to get rid of such an absurd law.
They ought to ... .

10 We must manage without a holiday this year.
We must ... .

Pause for thought

Is there a creature left over from the age of the dinosaurs living at the bottom of Loch Ness in Scotland?

Scientists say that it is possible that *Nessie*, as the monster is called by the local people, really does exist. For over 1,500 years there have been stories about the mysterious Scottish loch. They tell of a huge creature with a long neck that terrifies local people. In recent years, fresh evidence has shown that something is happening at the bottom of Britain's most famous stretch of fresh water. For a long time, scientists thought that the bottom of the loch, shut off from the sea at the end of the last Ice Age over 10,000 years ago, was lifeless. Now they know that, because of the unusually cold water 220 metres down, there are more than thirty types of creature in its depths.Researchers have recently detected strong bleeps in the loch on sonar equipment which tracks down underwater objects. It is also known for certain that there is enough food in the loch to feed a large creature.

There have been many reported sightings and even photographs of a huge animal with a long neck, but scientists are still looking for more conclusive evidence. Bones, skin and other remains are what are needed if the Loch Ness mystery is ever to be solved.

11

Spotlight on completion

Fill each of the numbered blanks in the following passage. Use only one word in each space.

In November 1872, the Mary Celeste (1) ... sail from New York with ten people on board. The ship was bound (2) ... Genoa, and the people on board were the captain, his wife and young daughter, and seven crewmen. (3) ... of these people survived the voyage, but (4) ... happened to them remains a complete mystery.

On the fourth of December, the small ship (5) ... sighted by a British ship, the Dei Gracia. Surprised to receive (6) ... answer to his signals, the captain of the Dei Gracia moved his ship closer to the Mary Celeste. Observing that there was (7) ... at the helm or (8) ... deck, he ordered some of his crew to row over to the ship and board her.

The British sailors (9) ... the ship from stem to stern, but the vessel was deserted. Why was the Mary Celeste sailing across the Atlantic (10) ... her crew? (11) ... strange had occurred, and yet everything seemed perfectly normal and (12) ... order. Breakfast was on the table in the captain's cabin though it (13) ... as if the meal had been abandoned halfway through. The deck had been washed, and clothes had been (14) ... out to dry. There was (15) ... of fresh food in the storeroom. The lifeboat was in (16) ... place, and the sails were undamaged.

No rational explanation seemed to fit the facts. If the crew members (17) ... been forced to leave the ship, they would (18)... used the lifeboat. If (19) ... had been a mutiny, some signs of disorder would have been found. If a storm had struck the ship, she would have been damaged in some way.

In the ship's log, the captain of the Mary Celeste had noted only routine details, (20) ... as weather conditions. According to one account of these events, the last sentence of the log was unfinished and began with the words: 'A strange thing is happening to us ... .'

Spotlight on spelling

Study the words for a minute. Then read out a word to a partner. Ask him or her to spell the word aloud. Check his or her spelling.

approach
association
disappointing
draught
drought
eventually
explanation
frequently
imaginative
improbable
incredible
marvellous
mysterious
nightmare
occurred
roughly
separated
unbelievable
unusually
wrinkled

Writing

Comment on a film you have seen, saying why you particularly liked or disliked it. (120 – 180 words)

Speaking

Look closely at this photograph which was taken inside a church. The photographer, Reverend K.F. Lord, vicar of this church, claims that he did not see the figure standing near the altar when he took this photograph.

1 Do you think that this photograph could be genuine or do you think it's definitely a fake?
2 What was your first reaction when you saw this photograph? Does the photograph make you feel uneasy?
3 Would you be prepared to spend a night on your own in this church with all the doors locked and the lights switched off?
4 Do you believe that some people – who claim to have psychic powers – can really predict the future or make contact with spirits?
5 What do you think of the horoscopes one finds in newspapers and magazines? Do you ever read them? Do you believe there is any truth in them?

11

Look at this photograph of a fortune-teller.

1 What would happen if you went to this woman for advice?
2 Would you ever go to a person like this for advice?
3 Do you believe that some people can see into the future?
4 Would you like to know what is going to happen to you?
5 What are your plans for the future?

Unit 12

Accuracy building 1

Choose the most appropriate word or phrase to complete each statement. After deciding which is the correct answer, focus your attention on the alternatives. When can they be used?

1 The sound is … . We'd better record that piece of music again.
a blurred *b* confused *c* distorted *d* deformed

2 By the time you … this letter, I shall be in Paris.
a will receive *b* will have received *c* receive *d* received

3 I hope you will not … a habit of turning up late.
a do *b* get *c* have *d* make

4 The clumsy waiter … some wine over my new dress.
a sprinkled *b* spilt *c* scattered *d* stained

5 Although my dog looks … , he's actually quite harmless.
a fierce *b* wildly *c* tame *d* savagely

6 We … as well go to Tom's party tonight. We have nothing better to do.
a might *b* must *c* could *d* should

7 The sun is getting into my eyes. Would you mind pulling down the … ?
a shutters *b* curtains *c* panes *d* blinds

8 I'm sorry. I mistook you … someone else.
a with *b* against *c* for *d* as

9 His … had always been to become a brain surgeon.
a want *b* ambition *c* temptation *d* request

10 Will you … me to the station?
a join *b* accompany *c* lift *d* walk along

11 She was … of feeding her baby when the telephone rang.
a in the middle *b* halfway through *c* midway *d* at the centre

12 I can't … you much about Mr Agnew as I hardly know him.
a talk *b* speak *c* say *d* tell

13 There's a storm approaching. We'd better take … somewhere.
a protection *b* safety *c* hiding *d* shelter

14 The early morning train was … with sleepy commuters.
a full *b* loaded *c* packed *d* overflowed

15 They found him … unconscious at the bottom of the stairs.
a lying *b* lain *c* laying *d* laid

16 I know this part of the city like the back of my … .
a leg *b* neck *c* head *d* hand

17 We were all tired from the long journey and, after a quick … , went straight to bed.
a feast *b* sandwiches *c* food *d* snack

18 I only managed to catch a brief … of the thief as he ran past me.
a glance *b* sight *c* glimpse *d* look

19 Please do not give the child any more sweets. You will only … him.
a damage *b* mistreat *c* worsen *d* spoil

20 It's a depressing day. It's cold and the sky's … .
a downcast *b* moody *c* overcast *d* despondent

21 A … year has 366 days.
a leap *b* jump *c* skip *d* hop

22 It's rather … outside. I think you should wear a scarf this morning.
a chilly *b* freezing *c* scorching *d* humid

23 At low … the sea goes out and that's when we can walk safely along the shore.
a dawn *b* level *c* dusk *d* tide

24 My brother works … a farm.
a in *b* on *c* at *d* for

25 I'm busy right now. I'll … to it later.
a deal *b* see *c* handle *d* mend

Accuracy building 2

Now complete the following statements from memory. Do not look back at the previous exercise.

1 The announcement over the loudspeaker was so … that I couldn't make out what was being said.
2 I will be in London by the time you … this letter.
3 I hope he will not … a habit of it.
4 It's no good crying over … milk!
5 I decided not to approach the … -looking dog.
6 We … as well try. After all, we have nothing to lose.
7 Office windows tend to have … rather than curtains.
8 I'm often mistaken … my twin brother.
9 His … is to climb Mt Everest.
10 He said he would … me home.
11 We were … of an important meeting when the fire alarm went off.
12 Now please … us a little bit about yourself.
13 You should not take … under a solitary tree during a thunder-storm.
14 The room was … with people anxious to hear him speak.
15 She spent the afternoon … on the beach.
16 I know this area like the back of my … .
17 Usually I just have a quick … for lunch.
18 Despite the crowds, I managed to catch a … of the Queen as she passed by.
19 You will only … your child if you give him everything he asks for.
20 The sky is … and there is a cold wind blowing.
21 Look before you … !
22 Wrap yourself up well. It's … outside.
23 The … came in and left the two boys stranded on the rocks.
24 Last year we spent two weeks … a farm in Wales.
25 I promise I'll … to it as soon as I can.

12

Spotlight on gerund or infinitive (2)

Finish each of the following sentences in such a way that it means exactly the same as the sentence printed above it.

Please speak more slowly.
Would you mind *speaking more slowly*?

1 Driving while under the influence of alcohol is a criminal offence.
It is ... .

2 Speaking with your mouth full is very bad manners.
It's ... .

3 I was present as a witness when he shot his wife.
I saw ... .

4 Somebody was coming up the stairs, so he switched off the light and hid under the bed.
He heard ... .

5 I was there when she took some money from the till.
I saw ... .

6 She slapped him across the face and then wished she hadn't done so.
She regretted ... .

7 'I didn't steal the necklace,' she said.
She denied ... .

8 He said he wouldn't hand over the document.
He refused ... .

9 He didn't keep his promise.
He failed ... .

10 I'll kill you if you don't follow my instructions!
He threatened ... .

11 Be careful! Don't touch that wire!
He warned me ... .

12 I'm very sorry to trouble you at this time of night, but I think you ought to know what has happened.
I hate ... .

13 If there's one thing I dislike intensely it's having to get up early on a cold wintry morning.
I hate ... .

14 I wouldn't go and see the film if I were you.
In my opinion, the film is not worth ... .

15 To discuss the matter with him would be a waste of time.
There's no point ... .

16 I am going to do my duty and nothing is going to stop me.
Nothing is going to prevent ... .

17 In order not to upset her, he didn't mention what had happened.
To avoid ... .

18 It's risky. You might lose everything.
You risk ... .

12

19 Have you ever thought it would be a good idea to work abroad?
Have you ever considered ... ?

20 Let's go out for a drink.
How ... ?

21 I was just about to say something when I noticed my boss at the other end of the room.
I was on the ... .

22 I wouldn't like to live anywhere else. I'm very happy where I am now.
I can't imagine ... .

23 What made him react so violently?
What caused ... ?

24 I was forced to leave my country.
I didn't choose ... .

25 I've been painting the room and now I've finished.
I've finished ... .

Reading

Read the passage below. Following the passage, you will find five unfinished statements. Decide which of the alternatives, *a*, *b*, *c* or *d*, best completes each statement.

PASSPORT TO ETERNITY

Two hundred years from now, Alan Sinclair expects to be out and about shopping, visiting the cinema and drinking in his local public house with his wife and eldest son.

He has joined delegates and scientists from across Europe and the United States for the first European Cryonics Conference which opens today at Gatwick. They will discuss topics such as the legal status of being frozen before clinical death and techniques to preserve tissue without damaging ice-crystal formation. Being frozen while healthy, they believe, could increase chances of a successful resurrection.

A fit-looking computer engineer, aged fifty-two, from near Eastbourne, Mr Sinclair has put £300,000 towards establishing a freezing facility near Gatwick, which he believes will be a passport to a kind of eternity. When the doctors pronounce Mr Sinclair clinically dead, he will be sent to Gatwick where his corpse will be pumped with preservative fluids and frozen in liquid nitrogen. Some twenty-four hours later his body will be in the Alcor Life Extension Foundation based in Riverside, California, after a flight in a specially designed cabinet.

When medical science and technology have advanced sufficiently, Mr Sinclair believes that he and his family will be brought back to life. 'It is a gamble, but I believe a realistic one given the way technology is advancing,' Mr Sinclair said.

'I do not think there is much choice. I may need a heart transplant one day and it might work, but there will come a time when medicine can do nothing and once you are buried or cremated, that's it.'

Before approaching insurance agents for a policy to cover the $120,000 (£61,000) needed for a whole-body freeze, Mr Sinclair consulted three British doctors on issues of clinical death and the preservation procedures used by American organisations offering eternity services, Alcor, Trans Times and the Cryonics Institute. They all felt it was futuristic but believed it might have a chance.

Mike Darwin, director of research at Alcor, said that the increasing interest in Europe and the more relaxed laws in Britain made it likely that European members would be stored at Gatwick by the turn of the century rather than in California. He talks of the service being an unorthodox method of patient care capable of cutting hospital waiting lists.

'Two thirds of the health care budget in the United States is spent on treating the terminally ill in their last six months. It is an appalling waste of resources,' he said.

Mr Sinclair has opted for a whole-body freeze because 'I liked the idea of being a good-looking corpse,' but many of the one hundred and ninety American and some of the twelve British members who have signed up have chosen to have their heads frozen for just $45,000.

They believe that emerging technologies will be able to mend damaged cells and clone back the person's body from brain cells.

Mr Darwin claims older people could, for example, have the choice of having longer legs or the physique of an international football player.

Over the next few days, delegates will discuss the legal status of being frozen before clinical death. They will consider the case of Dr Thomas Donaldson, aged forty-six, a mathematician from Sunnyvale, California, who has filed a lawsuit in America for the right to 'Cryonic suspension' before death.

He suffers from an incurable brain tumour which could kill him in five years and cause irreparable damage, limiting his chances of a successful resurrection, it is claimed.

(from an article in *The Times*)

1 According to the passage, Alan Sinclair
a has set up a freezing facility near Gatwick so that his corpse can be preserved until it can be brought back to life.
b plans to have his frozen corpse buried in Riverside, California.
c wishes to live for another two hundred years.
d expects to return to normal family life within two centuries or so.

2 Alan Sinclair
a is interested in cryonics because he is ill and needs a heart transplant.
b believes that medical science and technology have advanced sufficiently for him and his family to be brought back to life after they have died.
c obviously doesn't believe in a spiritual life after death.
d has paid insurance agents £61,000 for a whole-body freeze.

3 According to Mike Darwin,
a Cryonics will cure people who are terminally ill.
b more money should be spent on treating the terminally ill in their last six months.
c the eternity service offered by Alcor could result in a reduction in the number of patients waiting for hospital treatment.
d Alcor is taking an increasing interest in Europe where the laws - especially in Britain - are more relaxed than in the United States.

4 It would seem
a that the majority of American and British members have chosen to have just their heads frozen.
b that some people believe that - with the aid of technology - their brain cells will provide them with a new body when they are brought back to life.
c that you can freeze three heads for the price of one frozen body.
d that only good-looking people opt for a whole-body freeze.

5 Dr Thomas Donaldson
a believes he has the right to be frozen before he is pronounced clinically dead by doctors.
b has asked the delegates at the conference to consider his case.
c has been taken to court in America because of his insistence on his right to 'cryonic suspension' before death.
d suffers from a brain injury that cannot be treated.

12

Spotlight on vocabulary: health

Answer each question. Then discuss the difference between the words or phrases in italics. Give examples.

1 In an emergency, would you *send for* or *call on* a doctor?
2 Does an epidemic *break out* or *set out*?
3 If somebody has recovered from an illness, has that person *got over* or *come round* from the illness?
4 Do people *come up with* or *go down with* flu?
5 If you cut your finger, will it *bleed* or *swell*?
6 If you have cut your finger, will the cut eventually *cure* or *heal*?
7 Is an injured person carried to and from an ambulance on a *stretcher* or in a *hammock*?
8 Is a broken arm put *in stitches* or *in plaster*?
9 If you have spent all day on your feet, will your feet be *sore* or *sour*?
10 Having chopped wood all day with an axe, would you expect to find *blisters* or *freckles* on your hands?
11 Is a doctor's consulting-room and dispensary called a *surgery* or a *ward*?
12 Do doctors write out *recipes* or *prescriptions*?
13 Does exercise *make* or *do* you good?
14 If you are ill, are you *unfit* or *unwell*?
15 Do smokers tend to *cough* or *limp* a lot?
16 If you are in agony, are you in *grave* or *severe* pain?
17 If somebody has fainted, has that person *passed out* or *passed away*?
18 If you needed to have your eyes examined, would you consult an *optician* or a *physiotherapist*?
19 If you are travelling abroad, is it sensible to take a *vaccination* or a *first aid kit* with you?
20 Before putting a plaster on a cut, would you clean the wound with *cotton wool* or a *bandage*?

Spotlight on word formation: nouns

Complete each statement with an appropriate noun formed from the adjective or verb in the right-hand column.

1	Everybody was impressed by his … .	generous
2	Has that satisfied your … ?	curious
3	It has caused me a great deal of … .	anxious
4	He is a famous … .	invent
5	My driving … is very patient with me.	instruct
6	You didn't follow the … .	instruct
7	She works as a … in a restaurant.	wait
8	He is a lift … .	attend
9	I am seeking … .	employ
10	He has just dismissed three of his … .	employ
11	We can't interview every … for the job.	apply
12	Please fill in this … form.	apply
13	Have you got any form of … ?	identify
14	How much is the … fee?	admit
15	I'd like to give you a piece of … .	advise
16	The next … session will be on Thursday.	practise
17	He spoke at great … .	long
18	There is a … of water at the moment.	short
19	I'm out of my … .	deep
20	He doesn't know his own … .	strong

Have a laugh

'If you were my husband I'd poison your coffee,' Lady Astor told Sir Winston Churchill during one of the many rows they had.
'If you were my wife, I'd drink it,' he told her.

21 It's worth its ... in gold. weigh
22 He is of average ... . high
23 He measured the ... of the door. wide
24 He married her for her ... . beautiful
25 She married him for his ... . wealthy

Spotlight on phrasal verbs

Using *fall* or *get*, complete each sentence with a phrasal verb so that it means exactly the same as the sentence printed above it. You will need to use the following words: *away, back, by, down, for, off, on, out, round, through, to* and *with*.

I am not on friendly terms with my boss.
I don't *get on with my boss.*

1 Do you have any savings you can use in an emergency?
Do you have any savings you can ... ?

2 There is less demand for their products this year.
Demand for their products has ... .

3 I fell in love with her the moment I saw her.
I ... .

4 He quarrelled with his best friend.
He ... .

5 My plans have failed to materialise.
My plans ... .

6 How is he progressing in his new job?
How is he ... ?

7 The thieves escaped in a stolen car.
The thieves ... .

8 She has to manage on £40 a week.
She has to ... .

9 When will you find time to mend the fuse?
When will you ... ?

10 Don't let it depress you.
Don't let it ... .

11 He is nearly sixty.
He is ... .

12 I phoned several times, but I couldn't reach him.
I phoned several times, but I couldn't ... .

Spotlight on completion

Fill each of the numbered blanks in the following passage. Use only one word in each space.

(1) ... were many crazy and cruel rulers of ancient Rome, but none as eccentric as the Emperor Elagabalus. He became Emperor (2) ... the age of fourteen, and behaved in (3) ... a shocking manner that his own grandmother (4) ... him killed when he was just seventeen. She ordered his bodyguards to murder him and to throw his (5) ... into the

Tiber. So unpopular had the Emperor (6) ... that the soldiers (7) ... out the orders without hesitation.
Elagabalus loved (8) ... practical jokes, and it did not bother him if people died as a (9) ... of his jokes. On one (10) ..., he showered his dinner guests with rose petals. So (11) ... petals were used that some of the guests suffocated.
On other occasions he served his guests with artificial food (12) ... of glass or marble, (13) ... they had to eat. Even when real food was served, the Emperor's guests (14) ... often find spiders and flies mixed up in the food.
The Emperor's public appearances were also (15) ... unusual. He would sometimes arrive at a state function in a chariot (16) ... by lions or tigers.
Totally irresponsible, Elagabalus devoted (17) ... his time (18) ... the pursuit of pleasure. He ordered a magnificent bath to be built, used it once and (19) ... had it demolished. Fond (20) ... giving presents, he would often hide scorpions or poisonous snakes inside the presents he sent.

Spotlight on spelling

Study the words for a minute. Then read out a word to a partner. Ask him or her to spell the word aloud. Check his or her spelling.

accompany
announcement
appalling
eccentric
liquid
magnificent
majority
mathematician
medicine
optician
physique
poisonous
prescription
progressing
quarrelled
regretted
sufficiently
thieves
threatened
vaccination

Pause for thought

What is the origin of the simile
as mad as a hatter?

Until just before the Industrial Revolution, hats for men were made almost exclusively from animal skins. In preparing leather from animal hides, mercury, a silvery white, liquid metal, was extensively used.

Hatmakers, handling furs many hours a day over a period of years, gradually absorbed the poisonous metal which acted on the nervous system. As a result, many hatters became mentally disturbed as they grew older.

Writing

'I find television very educational. The minute somebody turns it on, I go to the library and read a good book.' (Groucho Marx)
'Television is a device that permits people who don't have anything to do, to watch people who can't do anything.' (Fred Allen)
Discuss the benefits and disadvantages of having a television in the home. (120 – 180 words)

12

Speaking

1 Comment on the photograph on this page.
2 Do you have any strong views on cosmetics? Do women spend too much money on make-up? Do you think men would look nicer if they wore make-up?
3 What do you think of people who have plastic surgery just to improve their looks? If you could afford it, would you pay to have your physical appearance changed by surgery?

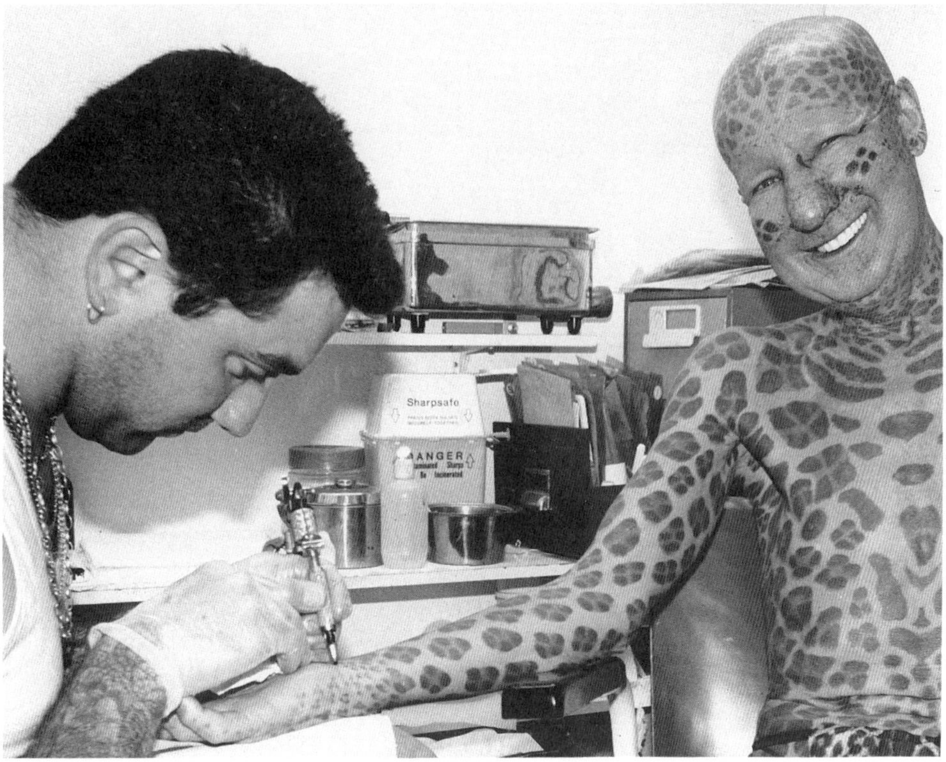

12

Look at the photograph above.

1 Describe what is happening in the photograph. Why, for example, is the boy on the right dressed in a white coat?
2 If you had a pet animal that was ill, what would you do?
3 If you could have any animal in the world as a pet, which one would you choose and why?
4 What were your favourite games as a child?
5 When was the last time you entered a toy shop? What did you buy and for whom?

Unit 13

Accuracy building 1

Choose the most appropriate word or phrase to complete each statement. After deciding which is the correct answer, focus your attention on the alternatives. When can they be used?

1 The hotel … Hyde Park.
a views *b* overlooks *c* opposes *d* is faced with

2 All of a sudden, the lights … out.
a put *b* switched *c* went *d* turned

3 To his astonishment, he was … the first prize.
a presented *b* won *c* awarded *d* rewarded

4 Not enough people stand … their rights.
a for *b* in for *c* up to *d* up for

5 I've just received an important … .
a information *b* news *c* message *d* advice

6 I am very concerned … your health. Please see a doctor.
a with *b* about *c* of *d* by

7 I'm looking forward … your brother.
a to meeting *b* to meet *c* meet *d* of meeting

8 I feel … .
a sleepy *b* asleep *c* sleeping *d* sleepless

9 She … her son for making a mess in his room.
a was punished *b* neglected *c* scolded *d* complained

10 After the match, the fans … out of the stadium.
a left *b* poured *c* departed *d* set

11 A clock has a face and two … .
a arms *b* needles *c* hands *d* arrows

12 I'm going to … my house to some students while I am abroad next year.
a let *b* hire *c* rent *d* borrow

13 He laughed so heartily at my joke that he dropped his glass, which … around his feet.
a scattered *b* creaked *c* shattered *d* cracked

14 She was … of all her savings.
a robbed *b* burgled *c* mugged *d* stolen

15 … you do, don't press that button.
a However *b* Whenever *c* Whoever *d* Whatever

16 He … with laughter.
a roared *b* growled *c* squeaked *d* grinned

17 Could you help me? I can't make head nor … of this.
a sense *b* tail *c* bottom *d* heels

18 We were not moving at all. The traffic had come to a complete … .
a standstill *b* jam *c* congestion *d* stationary

19 She is a … girl. I'm sure she'll not do anything foolish.
a sensitive *b* senseless *c* sensational *d* sensible

20 As we had missed the last bus, we … a lift from a passing motorist.
a hiked *b* hitched *c* gave *d* picked

21 I'm not wearing my watch because the … is broken.
a belt *b* string *c* band *d* strap

22 She burst … tears.
a in *b* out *c* out of *d* into

23 Caught out in the rain without an umbrella, I got … to the skin.
a absorbed *b* soaked *c* damp *d* wet

24 The editor decided to send his most experienced reporter to … the event.
a cover *b* write *c* comment *d* consider

25 Dinosaurs have been … for millions of years.
a disappearing *b* vanishing *c* extinct *d* extinguished

Accuracy building 2

Now complete the following statements from memory. Do not look back at the previous exercise.

1 The hotel … the sea.
2 There was a power cut and all the lights … out.
3 She was … a prize at school for good behaviour.
4 You should stand … what you believe in.
5 He is not in. Can I take a … ?
6 She is concerned … her son's behaviour.
7 I know she is looking forward … you.
8 This hot weather makes me feel … .
9 The child was … for getting his clothes dirty.
10 After the show, the crowd … out of the theatre.
11 The … on that clock are made of gold.
12 Do you have any property to … in this area?
13 As soon as I saw the … windscreen, I realised that my car had been vandalised.
14 He was … of all his money.
15 … you do, don't touch that wire.
16 He took one look at me and … with laughter.
17 I'm afraid I can't make head nor … of it.
18 The workers have gone on strike, so production has come to a … .
19 That was not very … of you. In fact, what you did was extremely silly.
20 I … a lift from London to Manchester.
21 It's a nice watch, but it needs a new … .
22 It was all too much for him and he burst … tears.
23 She got … to the skin.
24 There is nobody to … the event. Will you go?
25 Many species of animals are in danger of becoming … .

13

Spotlight on time constructions (1)

Finish each sentence in such a way that it means exactly the same as the sentence above it.

I arrived at five o'clock. I've *been here since five o'clock.*

1 Michael started collecting stamps ten years ago.
Michael has … .

2 I was given this watch on my fifteenth birthday.
I've … .

3 She learned to play the violin when she was eight.
She has … .

4 How long have you been smoking?
When … ?

5 He stopped eating meat five years ago.
He hasn't … .

6 I have been driving since the age of eighteen.
I learned … .

7 I haven't been to the theatre for ten years.
It's … .

8 I haven't seen a good film for ages.
It's … .

9 I have been working for this company for over thirty years.
It's … .

10 I haven't seen her for ten years now.
The … .

11 You haven't written to me since January.
The … .

12 When did they move to Scotland?
How long is … ?

13 When did you last go to the dentist?
How long is … ?

14 The first time I met her was at a fancy-dress party.
I … .

15 He has never been late before.
It's … .

16 I have never seen him in such a foul mood before.
It's … .

17 I plan to stay in France for three months.
I plan to spend … .

18 We lay on the beach the whole day.
We spent … .

19 I spent two hours writing that composition.
It took … .

20 It took him twenty minutes to cycle to work.
He cycled … .

13

Spotlight on word formation: nouns

Complete each statement with an appropriate noun formed from the adjective or verb in the right-hand column.

1	Most fires are started through … .	careless
2	As a businessman, he was a complete … .	fail
3	I wish people would respect my … .	private
4	They lived in … for many years.	poor
5	She has learnt to overcome her … .	shy
6	He is keen on … .	photograph
7	He is an amateur … .	photograph
8	He was declared the … .	win
9	He is suffering from … of memory.	lose
10	I asked my bank manager for a … .	lend
11	He has no sense of … .	responsible
12	I've decided to go in for that … .	compete
13	One of our business … has gone bankrupt.	compete
14	Do you have any … ? A son? A daughter?	depend
15	His … is very poor.	pronounce
16	Could you help me? I need some … .	assist
17	There is no … between the two.	compare
18	Fortunately, she has made a complete … .	recover
19	She asked him for an … .	explain
20	… is the mother of invention.	necessary
21	I don't have any … .	choose
22	I wish to make a … .	complain
23	I couldn't bear the … .	hot
24	He carried out his … .	threaten
25	To what … can he be trusted?	extend

Reading

Read the passage below. Following the passage, you will find five unfinished statements. Decide which of the alternatives, *a*, *b*, *c* or *d*, best completes each statement.

QUEEN OF ROMANCE

Lilo Militello, owner of the Concordia Notte restaurant in Paddington, was wearing a pink stetson hat to host his private lunch for Barbara Cartland and sixty of her most intimate friends.

It was supposed to be a celebration to mark the completion of her 500th novel but in the six weeks it took to organise the event, Barbara had produced another three. In fact, a total of 526 Cartland romances have actually been published. 'She loses count,' said PR Terri Baker. 'After all, she has sold 625 million copies in twenty-six languages.' Which probably explains why no one could remember the title of her latest book.

'No, I haven't a clue,' said Ian McCorquodale, Barbara's son and head of Cartland enterprises. 'You see, I read them in batches of twenty.'

Miss Cartland, as she prefers to be known, although she has been married twice, arrived in her white Mercedes (registration number BC29).

Each man was buttonholed with a pink carnation while their female partners were blamed for everything that is wrong with modern society. 'Any young man who gets married these days wants his head examining, the divorce laws are so awful. Half of everything he owns gets split up even if the woman is the guilty party.

'Now listen to this, it's important,' she continued, clawing at a male reporter's arm. 'Women can't have it all. If they want to have children, they should stay at home. Four out of five marriages fail, I know because I checked the figures.'

The secret of her success, she went on, was that all her heroines are virgins who never give way to temptation until their wedding night. They are also all blonde, like Miss Cartland was fifty years ago. Now her wavy hair is almost translucent and her make-up looks fit for an amateur pantomime.

'I say a prayer to get a plot, then I lie on the sofa and shut my eyes,' she continued. She then dictates to her secretary from 1pm to 3pm. 'Then I've done a chapter,' she explained. 'I do a book in fourteen days. If I didn't work, I'd die of boredom. So many of my contemporaries have gone senile.'

Various celebrities filed in until Mr Militello announced that 'Fillet of Sole alla BC' was served. Prince Michael received a round of applause for arriving late en route from the Dorchester hotel and Sir John Mills was heard to murmur, 'What are we here for?'

Squeezed into a pink Norman Hartnell creation topped with a huge cherry-red feather, Miss Cartland pecked like a huge exotic bird at the pink potatoes. Aged eighty-nine and a self-appointed authority on alternative medicine, she is still a good advertisement for honey and answers thirty thousand letters a year on health matters.

Finally it was on to the musical tribute. She was moved to tears when all the men stood up to sing *If You Were the Only Girl in the World.*

(from an article in *The Guardian*)

1 Miss Barbara Cartland
a has published 625 million copies of her novels throughout the world.
b is a celebrated writer of romantic fiction.
c has written so many novels that even her son doesn't know the exact number.
d has written 526 romances in twenty-six languages.

2 According to Miss Cartland,
a four out of five marriages fail because women today do not stay at home to look after their children.
b the secret of her success lies in the fact that all the principal characters in her books have high moral standards.
c any young man who gets married these days must be crazy.
d the present divorce laws are awful because they encourage women to be unfaithful.

3 It takes Miss Cartland
a a couple of hours to write a chapter.
b a fortnight to complete a book.
c about a month to produce three books.
d three hours to dictate a chapter to her secretary.

4 We gather from the passage that Miss Cartland
a wears little make-up and that her favourite colour is pink.
b has medical qualifications and gives advice on health matters.
c eats honey, which apparently does her good.
d will only eat food that has been coloured pink.

5 The passage informs us that
a many of Miss Cartland's friends have gone senile.
b Miss Cartland was visibly upset when all the men stood up to sing If You Were the Only Girl in the World.
c Miss Cartland wore a tight pink dress wrapped in a huge cherry-red feather.
d Miss Cartland would find life unbearably tedious if she stopped working.

Spotlight on vocabulary: relationships

Answer each question. Then discuss the difference between the words or phrases in italics. Give examples.

1 Do parents *bring up* or *grow up* their children?
2 Peter is Mary's cousin. Is Peter *related* or a *relative* to Mary?
3 If Teresa is your cousin, is she *familiar* to you or a *relation* of yours?
4 Mary's sister has a daughter called Michelle. Is Michelle Mary's *niece* or *nephew*?
5 Mary's father died a few years ago and Mary's mother is now married to a man called Bill. Is he Mary's *godfather* or *stepfather*?
6 Mary's sister is married to Thomas. Is he Mary's *uncle* or *brother-in-law*?
7 Ronald's wife died last year. Is he a *widow* or a *widower*?
8 Andrew is single. Is he a *spinster* or a *bachelor*?
9 Yesterday Andrew proposed to Julie. Did he ask her for a *date* or for her *hand in marriage*?
10 Julie turned Andrew down. Did she *accept* or *reject* his proposal?
11 Andrew is very upset because Julie will not marry him. Has Julie hurt Andrew's *heart* or *feelings*?
12 If somebody is important to you, do you care *of* or *about* that person?
13 Carol is getting married next month. Will she be the *bride* or *groom*?
14 After a wedding are the guests usually invited to a *reception* or a *folk-dance*?
15 Mr and Mrs Brown are no longer living together. Are they living *separately* or *apart*?
16 Barbara has gone off John. Does that mean she has *run away with him* or that she has *lost interest in him*?
17 You wish to celebrate your birthday with your friends. Would you *make* or *give* a party?
18 Are you more likely to receive letters from a *pen pal* or a *classmate*?
19 If somebody has just deliberately ignored you, have you been given the *cold shoulder* or a *warm welcome*?
20 If two people are madly in love, are they *crazy* or *very fond* about each other?

Spotlight on phrasal verbs

Using *go*, complete each sentence with a phrasal verb so that it means exactly the same as the sentence printed above it. You will need to use the following words: *after*, *back*, *by*, *for*, *in*, *off*, *on*, *out*, *over*, *round*, *through* and *with*.

She has fallen ill with flu.
She has *gone down with flu*.

1 The milk has turned sour.
The milk … .

2 I've decided to enter that particular competition.
I've decided … .

3 The fire alarm sounded and we all left the building.
The fire alarm … .

4 Those trousers don't match your jacket.
Those trousers don't … .

5 The fire stopped burning.
The fire … .

6 Please continue, I'm listening.
Please … .

7 I chased the thief but he escaped.
I … .

8 He broke his promise.
He … .

9 Time passes quickly when you are enjoying yourself.
Time … .

10 The bomb exploded and killed three people.
The bomb … .

11 We need to examine the accounts.
We need … .

12 I hope there will be enough food for everybody.
I hope there will be enough food … .

13 Make sure you practise these phrasal verbs.
Make sure you … .

14 The dog attacked the postman.
The dog … .

Have a laugh

A musician stood in the middle of the jungle, playing a flute beautifully. One by one animals came from all parts of the jungle and sat down to listen to the music. Tigers, snakes, elephants, even the fiercest animals were soothed by the music. Suddenly, a lion walked up to the musician and ate him.
'What on earth did you do that for?' asked a leopard. 'He was playing so beautifully.'
The lion put his hand to his ear and said, 'What?'

Spotlight on completion

Fill each of the numbered blanks in the following passage. Use only one word in each space.

A famous general had a grand-daughter of (1) … he was very fond. One day he (2) … her to the circus, where they saw all the things (3) … children love (4) … much. There were elephants, lions and tigers, and animals of (5) … kind. But (6) … interested the little girl most (7) … the clown, who happened to have the same first name (8) … the general. The little girl was so amused by Horace's tricks (9) … when she went home again she (10) … her mother all about them. The mother was very surprised to hear the child call her grandfather (11) … his first name, as she thought, but she was (12) … more astonished when she learnt (13)… the extraordinary things which the old man was said to (14) … done. When the child told her at last how Horace had fallen into a bucket of flour, she (15) … that she had made a mistake and laughed heartily (16) … the joke. Seeing her father the next day, she could not (17) … asking him (18) … he had felt when he was covered (19) … flour. The general looked puzzled (20) … he realised what had happened, and then he too roared with laughter at the mistake.

13

Spotlight on spelling

Study the words for a minute. Then read out a word to a partner. Ask him or her to spell the word aloud. Check his or her spelling.

absorbed	relief
boredom	roared
creaked	shattered
eight	soaked
extraordinary	stunned
extremely	supposed
fifteenth	tedious
grinned	theatre
neglected	thoughtful
preparation	unbearably

Writing

Men and women will never be equal, for they have different responsibilities and different roles to play in society. Discuss. (120 –180 words)

Pause for thought

What is the origin of the term *male chauvinist*?

Nicholas Chauvin was a soldier during the French Revolution at the end of the 18th century. Later, he served under Napoleon and was awarded medals for his bravery. However, he made such a fuss about his love of France and his admiration for Napoleon that people began to mock him.

Soon Chauvin's name came to mean anyone who was blindly devoted to a cause. In the 1960s, feminists used the term *male chauvinist* to describe men who only saw things from the point of view of their own sex.

Speaking

1 Comment on each of the photographs in turn. Which one do you find the most romantic?
2 Do you enjoy reading romantic stories or watching romantic films?
3 What is your reaction to advertisements that use romantic images to promote products? Are you influenced by such advertisements?
4 If a man takes a woman out to dinner, do you think he should pay for the meal?
5 Women are supposed to be more romantic than men. Do you agree?

Unit 14

Accuracy building 1

Choose the most appropriate word or phrase to complete each statement. After deciding which is the correct answer, focus your attention on the alternatives. When can they be used?

1 She reminds me … someone I knew many years ago.
a for *b* to *c* about *d* of

2 Mr Smith would not … to my marrying his daughter.
a consent *b* allow *c* let *d* permit

3 … you see Ronald tonight, please tell him to give me a ring.
a Happen *b* Would *c* Will *d* Should

4 I shall go ahead … of the consequences.
a despite *b* regardless *c* whatever *d* no matter

5 I'd like to take this opportunity to … my gratitude to you all.
a say *b* express *c* tell *d* speak

6 Be at my office at nine o'clock tomorrow morning without … .
a fail *b* missing *c* fault *d* failure

7 What … is he? Lieutenant or captain?
a grade *b* level *c* category *d* rank

8 I have been asked to write … of Arthur Thomson's latest novel.
a an article *b* a critic *c* a comment *d* a review

9 How much damage did the storm do … your roof?
a with *b* for *c* to *d* against

10 Would you mind not standing … the way?
a in *b* by *c* on *d* over

11 Although he found the situation amusing, he tried to keep a … face so as not to offend his host.
a rigid *b* stiff *c* straight *d* numb

12 He's so timid, he's even frightened of his own … !
a shade *b* shadow *c* figure *d* shape

13 You could set your watch by him. He's as … as clockwork.
a steady *b* true *c* regular *d* precise

14 The chair gave … under his weight and he ended up on the floor.
a up *b* way *c* off *d* out

15 Five … two equals ten.
a minus *b* times *c* plus *d* multiplied

16 There's far too much information for me to … in all at once.
a absorb *b* digest *c* take *d* retain

17 We intend to … the cottage to its original state.
a restore *b* renew *c* renovate *d* refurnish

18 The ship dropped … outside the port.
a sail *b* anchor *c* mast *d* funnel

19 I'll take care of this bill, and you can … up with me later.
a pay *b* owe *c* settle *d* cash

20 Young hooligans and teenage vandals are classed as juvenile … .
a criminals *b* delinquents *c* hoodlums *d* gangsters

21 You're … like a leaf. What's wrong?
a shaking *b* flapping *c* waving *d* rattling

22 Thomas … brilliantly in the exam. He obtained full marks.
a passed *b* did *c* acted *d* showed

23 I like to … a drink slowly, savouring its taste.
a gulp *b* swallow *c* sip *d* gargle

24 The robbery occurred in … daylight.
a wide *b* broad *c* full *d* plain

25 How clever of you! I'd never have … the answer if you hadn't told me.
a solved *b* thought *c* guessed *d* produced

Accuracy building 2

Now complete the following statements from memory. Do not look back at the previous exercise.

1 I must remind you … our agreement.
2 He would not … to her marrying such a man.
3 … you change your mind, don't hesitate to contact me.
4 We shall continue with our plans … of the expense involved.
5 I find it difficult to … my thoughts on paper.
6 I expect you to be here at eight o'clock without … .
7 He was promoted to the … of captain.
8 I think the play deserved a better … than it got in the local paper.
9 It was a minor accident. No damage was done … the car.
10 You can't put it there. It will be … everybody's way.
11 Despite his desire to laugh, he managed to keep a … face.
12 He's just a … of his former self.
13 He's as … as clockwork.
14 The shelf gave … under so much weight and sent the books crashing to the floor.
15 Twenty … five equals one hundred.
16 I was too tired to … in everything that he said.
17 It would be nice to … this house to its former beauty.
18 An … prevents a ship from drifting away.
19 Could you pay for me as well? I'll … up with you tomorrow.
20 If you send juvenile … to prison, most of them will end up as hardened criminals.
21 She was so frightened that she began … like a leaf.
22 She … quite well in the exam and was satisfied with the grade she obtained.
23 When it's very hot, I prefer to sit in the shade and … a nice cool drink.
24 It happened in … daylight with plenty of people about.
25 I have to admit that I … the answer.

14

Spotlight on time constructions (2)

Finish each sentence in such a way that it means exactly the same as the sentence above it.

Your bedtime was hours ago.
It's well *past your bedtime*.

1 He has written nineteen novels and will write one more before he retires.
By the time … .

2 I have been working for the same company for twenty-nine years, and next year will make it thirty.
By this time next year … .

3 I have been in England since last April.
By next April … .

4 By this time next year I shall have been teaching English at Felton College for twenty-eight years.
I have … .

5 The children put out the fire before the firemen arrived.
By the time … .

6 He became the company's top salesperson before the age of twenty.
By the time … .

7 She left for Italy before I received her letter.
By the time … .

8 Only later did I realise what a terrible mistake I had made.
I didn't … .

9 It was only when I opened my handbag that I discovered my credit cards had been stolen.
It wasn't … .

10 As soon as they arrived home, they started quarrelling.
No sooner … .

11 I have never been so insulted in all my life!
Never … !

12 We should leave. It's getting late.
It's time for … .

13 Why aren't you in bed? It's very late.
It's time you … .

14 You are taking too long to decide what to do.
It's about time you … .

15 He's too big for his boots. Someone ought to teach him a lesson.
It's high time he … .

16 The roof still needs repairing.
The roof hasn't … .

17 He's too busy to see you right now. He's showing a client around the factory.
He can't see you right now because he is busy … .

18 First we visited Tom and then we called in to see Ann.
After … .

19 Having done some shopping in Oxford Street, we went home.
Before … .

20 You have until Friday to complete the report.
The report … .

Spotlight on word formation: adjectives

Complete each statement with an appropriate adjective formed from the noun or verb in the right-hand column.

1	She's too … . She must learn not to trust everybody.	trust
2	You can trust him. He's both honest and … .	trust
3	He is an excellent worker. He is efficient and … .	rely
4	She is extremely … to criticism.	sense
5	It's not worth anything. It's … .	worth
6	We should support them. It's a … cause.	worth
7	His parents still support him. He's … on them.	depend
8	He's … . He won't let you down.	depend
9	It's a … film, one of the best of its kind.	class
10	I prefer listening to … music.	class
11	I can't go out like this. My hair is in a … mess.	fright
12	The present … situation is rather worrying.	economy
13	I'm looking for a car that's … to run.	economy
14	I prefer to buy … toys for my children.	education
15	The … chicken I bought needs defrosting.	freeze
16	How immature of him. He's so … .	child
17	The bored children started to grow … .	rest
18	We stood … as she drowned before our very eyes.	help
19	It's no good. I'm … at learning facts.	hope
20	I felt very sorry for him. He looked so … .	pity
21	It was an … experience. I shall always remember it.	forget
22	She has a poor memory. She is quite … at times.	forget
23	Apples are … this year.	plenty
24	He's a … person; so charming and witty.	delight
25	It can't be bought with money. It's … .	price

Reading

Read the passage below. Following the passage, you will find five unfinished statements. Decide which of the alternatives, *a*, *b*, *c* or *d*, best completes each statement.

PUBLIC ENTERTAINMENT

The Karaoke craze which has swept London is causing confusion at town halls throughout the capital.

With more pubs introducing the Japanese entertainment, where customers take to the stage and sing along to a machine playing the backing tracks of their favourite hits, the question of licensing has been raised.

When would-be Elvis Presleys and Madonnas grasp the microphone and croon to the amusement of their friends, they are technically performing live music.

Tower Hamlets Council has told publicans in the borough that if they install a Karaoke machine they must have a licence which authorises them to stage live performances or face a fine of £2000.

Chief trading standards officer Edward Lubbock said: 'Karaoke evenings are a lot of fun but when people crowd into a confined space and an emergency needs to be dealt with, it could prove fatal.'

By law publicans need a dance and music licence for discos, a cabaret licence for up to two performers on stage and a music licence for acts with more than two performers.

Michael Roxin, owner of Tipples in Bethnal Green Road, said nobody seemed to know how to categorise Karaoke. 'The town hall and the powers-that-be haven't worked out where it stands. I even went to see the police inspector to ask him if I needed a special licence and he said he didn't know.'

Watching a Karaoke evening, one can see the dilemma. It's like a disco, a cabaret, a pop concert and a private party rolled into one.

Theresa Monaf, aged twenty, still on a high after her performance of *So Emotional*, pointed out: 'Older people forget that in their day they used to have a sing-song in the pub with the piano. Now we sing along to computers and videos, it's no different.' She and her friends were shocked to hear that councils could clamp down on Karaoke.

Olivia Paden, a partner in the business Karaoke Knites which hires out equipment and comperes to landlords, said she had heard of pubs being asked to stop doing Karaoke because they did not have a licence.

'The trouble is that no one has ever gone to court over it, so it is difficult to tell what the exact position is,' she said. 'It would be a shame to clamp down. Singing brings people together and brings out the best in them.'

(From an article in the *London Evening Standard*)

1 Karaoke is a form of entertainment that
a has swept discos and nightclubs in London.
b has been banned in pubs.
c is enjoyed by older people who like to have a sing-song.
d has caused a certain amount of legal confusion.

2 A Karaoke evening would not be possible without
a a licence from the local council.
b electricity.
c people with good singing voices.
d a pub.

3 If a publican hires a performer to sing and dance on a stage, he will need
a a *music* licence.
b a *cabaret* licence.
c a *dance and music* licence.
d a *live performance* licence.

4 Karaoke
a combines various elements of more traditional forms of entertainment.
b is performed by professional singers.
c can be fatal.
d brings out the best in people.

5 It would seem that the principal objection to Karaoke is that
a a publican could be fined £2000.
b it encourages a party atmosphere in pubs.
c nobody seems to know how to categorise it.
d the machines are often installed in unsuitable places.

14

Spotlight on vocabulary: entertainment

Answer each question. Then discuss the difference between the words or phrases in italics. Give examples.

1 Do actors perform in front of *an audience* or *a congregation*?
2 Are you shown to your seat in a theatre by *a guide* or *an usherette*?
3 Are cinema seats arranged in *rows* or *files*?
4 Before a play is performed, do the actors *rehearse* or *repeat* their parts?
5 Is the final rehearsal of a play called the *dress* or *costume rehearsal*?
6 Is a film shown on a *stage* or a *screen*?
7 Does a set designer design the *scenery* or *landscape* for a play?
8 Do you *make* or *put on* a play?
9 Does an actor have to learn his *lines* or his *script*?
10 In a theatre, are refreshments served during the *interruption* or the *interval*?
11 Does an audience show its appreciation of a performance by *booing* or *clapping*?
12 Does the *director* or the *producer* tell the actors how they should play their parts?
13 Do you *shoot* or *stage* a film?
14 If you want better television reception, do you *remove* or *adjust* the aerial?
15 Does a television have different *canals* or *channels*?
16 Does a disc *announcer* or *jockey* play records in a discotheque?
17 Do the lights *flash* or *twinkle* when you dance in a disco?
18 Do *porters* or *bouncers* sort out any trouble in discos?
19 Are records recorded in a *box-office* or a *studio*?
20 If a record is a hit, is it a commercial *success* or *failure*?

Spotlight on phrasal verbs

Using *hand*, *hang* or *hold*, complete each sentence with a phrasal verb so that it means exactly the same as the sentence printed above it. You will need to use the following words: *about/around*, *back*, *down*, *in*, *on*, *out*, *over* and *up*.

Wait a moment, I'll see what I can do.
Hang on a moment, I'll see what I can do.

1 I forgot to give in my homework.
I forgot to ... .

2 Have you distributed all the leaflets?
Have you ... ?

3 Give me the money or I'll shoot you!
... !

4 He stamped my passport and then returned it to me.
He stamped my passport and then ... .

5 Please don't put down the receiver. What I have to say is very important.
Please don't ... .

6 There is a suspicious-looking man loitering near the entrance.
There is a suspicious-looking man ... .

Have a laugh

A man got into a taxi and asked the driver to take him to town. The driver agreed and sped off, quickly accelerating to 70 mph. The passenger said timidly, 'If possible, I want to get there safe and sound!'
The driver asked, 'Do you know how to handle this make of car?'
'No,' the passenger replied, and the driver said, 'Keep quiet then!'
Shortly afterwards, the speed climbed to 100 mph, and the passenger again said, 'Please I want to arrive safely.'
Again the driver asked, 'Do you know how to handle this car?' and again the passenger said he did not. But when the driver pushed the speed to 130 mph, the nervous passenger could not contain himself. 'I want to get there alive!' he shouted.
For the third time, the driver asked, 'Do you know how to handle this make of car?' This time, in desperation, the passenger said he did.
'All right,' the driver replied, 'could you tell me where the brake is?'

7 We were delayed by the traffic.
We were … .

8 Could you wait, please? I'll try and put you through.
Could you … .

9 Three banks have been robbed in the past two days.
Three banks have … .

10 He has never been able to keep a job for more than a couple of months.
He has never been able to … .

Spotlight on completion

Fill each of the numbered blanks in the following passage. Use only one word in each space.

While I was waiting for my brother (1) … the corner of the street, I saw a man (2) … out of a car and enter a narrow lane (3) … the other (4) … of the road. He was wearing a bowler (5) … and a black overcoat, and (6) … his hand was a small suitcase, (7) … he placed on the (8) … and opened. (9) … it he took a ragged coat and a dirty cap, and (10) … anyone but I could see him, he quickly put them on, leaving his other (11) … in the case. He then walked slowly out to the main road, sat down on the pavement and took (12) … his cap, which he left (13) … him. He (14) … exactly like a beggar, and indeed that was (15) … he was. I walked across the road and stood watching him (16) … my brother appeared, and during the quarter of an (17) … I was there more than twenty people (18) … to give him something. I told my brother what I had seen and we decided to speak to the man. (19) … our surprise, he immediately got up and ran as fast as he (20) … towards his car.

Spotlight on spelling

Study the words for a minute. Then read out a word to a partner. Ask him or her to spell the word aloud. Check his or her spelling.

accelerate	opportunity
agreement	partner
daughter	renovate
designer	straight
discotheque	technically
encourage	throughout
favourite	tomorrow
gratitude	travellers
immediately	unsuitable
licence	usherette

Pause for thought

Why does *to hold up* mean both *to rob* and *to delay*?

In the days when people used to travel on horse-back or by horse-drawn vehicles, it was often not safe to travel because of highwaymen. A highwayman was someone who used to rob travellers on public roads. He would order his victim to hold up his hands above his head to ensure that he was not reaching for a weapon. At the same time, the traveller would have had his journey delayed by the robbery.

14

Writing

Discuss the advantages and disadvantages of living in a large town or city. (120 – 180 words)

Speaking

1 Describe what is happening in this photograph.
2 Do you admire stuntmen for their skills and courage, or do you think that they are crazy to risk serious injury or even death just for the sake of entertaining the public?
3 What is the most spectacular stunt you have ever seen (either on film or in real life)?
4 Do you think that people who drive dangerously or under the influence of alcohol should be imprisoned?
5 What can be done to ease the present traffic problems in most towns and cities?

Unit 15

Accuracy building 1

Choose the most appropriate word or phrase to complete each statement. After deciding which is the correct answer, focus your attention on the alternatives. When can they be used?

1 The tunnel was so dark that he … a match to see where he was going.
a struck *b* set fire to *c* set alight *d* illuminated

2 I don't feel … to going to work today.
a as *b* up *c* like *d* down

3 He took a room in a boarding house … by a middle-aged couple.
a governed *b* ruled *c* run *d* directed

4 I was told to pack my … and leave the house.
a articles *b* belongings *c* pieces *d* objects

5 We'll have to buy a fresh loaf. This bread is … .
a mould *b* soft *c* stale *d* rusty

6 He went to a fancy-dress party … up as a pirate.
a disguised *b* concealed *c* pretending *d* dressed

7 She only has a small pension and finds it hard to make ends … .
a survive *b* tight *c* join *d* meet

8 The oil heater is … dangerous fumes. I think we'd better have it checked by an expert.
a giving off *b* consuming *c* contaminating *d* sending

9 Every tin should have a … stating what its contents are.
a lid *b* ladle *c* label *d* lapel

10 Having taken everything … account, we have decided not to accept the offer.
a in *b* on *c* for *d* into

11 I don't remember … that. I'm sure you are mistaken.
a say *b* saying *c* to say *d* to have said

12 In our back garden we have a … where we keep plants and grow tomatoes.
a shed *b* greenhouse *c* workshop *d* hut

13 They lowered the … into the grave.
a tomb *b* hearse *c* undertaker *d* coffin

14 They set … early the next morning.
a in *b* off *c* to *d* away

15 After many years of globe-trotting, he finally got married and settled … .
a home *b* for ever *c* down *d* for good.

16 No sooner had I opened the door … my wife started shouting at me.
a than *b* when *c* then *d* so

17 They … for a baby-sitter to come and look after their children.
a arranged *b* organised *c* prepared *d* requested

18 I've been stung by a bee. Have you got any … cream?
a antidote *b* skin *c* antiseptic *d* disinfectant

19 It's really dark outside. We'd better take a … with us.
a chandelier *b* torch *c* compass *d* lamp-post

20 She says she's feeling as fit as a … .
a fiddle *b* gymnast *c* ballerina *d* horse

21 A vacuum cleaner is a household … .
a machine *b* appliance *c* device *d* tool

22 I'd like to know the reason … his absence.
a of *b* about *c* for *d* why

23 Where on … have you been?
a earth *b* heaven's name *c* the blazes *d* wonder

24 If I were you, I'd take what he says with a … of salt.
a speck *b* pinch *c* measure *d* drop

25 What a … your sister is! She never stops talking.
a parrot *b* talkative *c* chatterbox *d* speaker

Accuracy building 2

Now complete the following statements from memory. Do not look back at the previous exercise.

1 He … a match and lit his cigarette.
2 I'd rather not go out for a walk. I don't really feel … to it.
3 The hotel is … by a close friend of mine.
4 He possesses very little. He has few … .
5 This sandwich is awful. The bread is … and the cheese is tasteless.
6 He … up as Father Christmas to amuse his children.
7 I don't know how we are going to make ends … .
8 Remove that at once! It's … a nasty smell.
9 That's my suitcase. My name and address are on the … .
10 You should take the following facts … account before making your decision.
11 Are you sure I said that? I honestly don't remember … that to you.
12 Plants that require a constant temperature are grown in a … .
13 The … was transported to the cemetery in a hearse.
14 They set … at dawn.
15 When are you going to get married and settle … ?
16 No sooner had he started to sing … the audience burst into applause.
17 I have … for the plumber to come round this afternoon.
18 You'd better put some … cream on that cut.
19 I can't see anything. Switch on your … .
20 Despite his old age, he's as fit as a … .
21 A kettle is an extremely useful household … .
22 He didn't give a reason … his sudden resignation.
23 What on … happened to you yesterday?
24 He tends to exaggerate. I'd take what he says with a … of salt if I were you.
25 What a … ! She never knows when to stop talking.

15

Spotlight on: *too, enough, so* and *such*

Finish each sentence in such a way that it means exactly the same as the sentence above it.

There's not enough salt in the soup.
There's too *little salt in the soup.*

1 This tea is too sweet.
There is too .... .

2 We need to put more petrol in the tank.
There is not .... .

3 She's too young to go out on her own.
She's not .... .

4 You should have tried harder.
You didn't .... .

5 I can't afford to buy you a decent present.
I don't .... .

6 It was so dark that we couldn't see where we were going.
It was too .... .

7 This book is too difficult for children to read.
It's too .... .

8 I was too frightened to say anything.
I was so .... .

9 The coffee was so hot I couldn't drink it.
The coffee was too .... .

10 The child is so spoilt that nobody likes her.
She is such .... .

11 We were so unlucky yesterday.
We had such .... .

12 I didn't realise the work would be so hard.
I didn't realise it would .... .

13 It was a very hot day, so we decided to go for a swim in the lake.
It was such .... .

14 I've got so many things to do this morning.
I've got such .... .

15 I see this student so rarely that I've forgotten his name.
So .... .

Have a laugh

Jock McTavish was really mean. He simply hated spending money. One day Jock asked a bus conductor how much the bus fare into the city was.
'Thirty pence,' said the conductor.
Jock thought this was a bit much, so he decided to run behind the bus for a few stops.
'How much is the fare now?' he panted, after running behind the bus for five minutes.
'Still thirty pence,' said the conductor.
Jock ran behind the bus for another five minutes. When the bus stopped, he was so worn out that he could hardly speak.
'How much is the fare now?' he gasped.
'Fifty pence,' said the conductor. 'You are running in the wrong direction.'

15

Spotlight on word formation: verbs

Complete each statement with an appropriate verb formed from the word given in the right-hand column.

1	It shouldn't have cost as much as that. He has … you.	charge
2	He was … for cheating in the race.	qualify
3	He's a naughty child. He's always … in class.	behave
4	The accident happened when the motorcyclist tried to … the lorry.	take
5	She … me for a friend of hers. In fact, I didn't know her at all.	take
6	Some adverts … the public with their false claims.	lead
7	I must have … her. I thought she said something else.	understand
8	Can you … the man who attacked you?	identity
9	I wish you would stop … me all the time.	critic
10	I'd like to have these photos … .	large
11	I'm sure he'll soon … his difficulties.	come
12	The wall needs … .	strong
13	He sent her roses and chocolates in an attempt to … her heart.	soft
14	The sleeves are too long. I'll have to … them.	short
15	The gap has … .	wide
16	His voice has … .	deep
17	I'm trying to … him from smoking.	courage
18	I'm trying to … him to take up a sport.	courage
19	She has … her glasses again. Could you help her look for them?	place
20	You've … the meat. It's been in the oven for too long.	cook
21	I was … by the loud noise.	deaf
22	The news … her.	sad
23	The screw needs … .	tight
24	The trousers felt tight round the waist so he … his belt.	loose
25	It is said that reading … one's mind.	broad

Reading

Read the passage below. Following the passage, you will find five unfinished statements. Decide which of the alternatives, *a*, *b*, *c* or *d*, best completes each statement.

WAITING TO PAY

It's the end of an enjoyable meal. Coffee has been served, the cups have been refilled and conversation slows down. It's time to pay and go.

But now comes the hard part. The previously attentive waiters suddenly disappear, or practise looking through you. Your feeling of well-being begins to evaporate as you struggle with the age-old problem: how do you pay your bill?

There are many time-honoured ruses for persuading a restaurant to take your money. The most universal is the beckoning movement (slight but rapid) of the forefinger in the air. It's a gesture recognised from the Far East to Land's End.

Another more modern technique is to place your plastic ostentatiously on the table. But that presupposes a waiter is moving in your direction in the first place. A third – often practised by considerate hosts who don't want their guests to know how much the meal cost – is to approach the head waiter and pay discreetly.

If all these methods fail, what do you do? For Tom Jaine, editor of the *Good Food Guide*, there is one simple answer. 'I get up, put on my coat and stand by the door. I pay the bill in no time at all.'

15

But why should a restaurant-goer have to resort to such devices? It often seems as if the restaurant is delighted to serve you, but is reluctant to deal with something as sordid as money. Or is it to do with the inability of waiting staff to spot the psychological moment of departure?

Half the pleasure in a restaurant meal derives from how it is served. More than just pretty plates, it involves the way the meal is paced. A waiter should be able to spot whether you are a party who wants to spend the whole evening over dinner or whether you're in a hurry. If it's lunch-time, eating will be quicker. Paying the bill is part of that pacing, and is the point where it often goes wrong.

Paying is also the moment when the customer returns to the real world. Michael Gill, who owns a restaurant, says: 'When people make the decision to go, they want to go fast. The trouble is, it's just at the moment when the customer snaps out of his relaxed mood that the restaurant staff begin to wind down at the end of lunch or dinner service.'

According to Tom Jaine, himself a former restaurateur, preparing bills is the part that gets forgotten. 'You work hard, getting the food to the tables at the right time, and then everybody wants to go at the same time, and there are no bills for them.' He suggests that restaurants should employ someone whose job is just to make out bills.

So perhaps restaurants should scrap expensive computers, employ an army of retired cashiers to make out bills and teach waiters to be discreetly at hand when we decide to go. I suppose we customers could also learn to ask for our bills in good time. But that's expecting a bit much, don't you think?

(adapted from an article in the *Weekend Telegraph*)

1 If you are in a hurry, the most effective way of attracting a waiter's attention is
a to make a rude gesture with your forefinger.
b to leave the restaurant without paying.
c to put your clothes on and stand by the door.
d to leave your table and make for the door.

2 The author mentions several techniques for persuading a restaurant to take your money. One of these is
a to call the head waiter.
b to draw attention to yourself by putting your hand up in the air.
c to pay beforehand so that your guests will not know how much the meal cost.
d to draw the waiter's attention to your credit card on the table.

3 According to the author of this passage,
a a waiter should be able to judge when it is the right moment to present the bill.
b waiters don't seem to understand human psychology.
c how a meal is served is more important than pretty plates on the table.
d a waiter should understand that everybody is in a hurry at lunch-time.

4 It is quite clear from this passage that most restaurant staff
a are lazy and inefficient.
b are far too relaxed and casual in the way they treat their customers.
c spend so much time and energy attending to the basic needs of their customers that they tend to overlook one final detail.
d are never in a hurry to prepare and present a bill because they regard money as something sordid.

5 The author of this passage thinks that it would be unrealistic to expect
a restaurants to replace their expensive computers with an army of retired cashiers.
b customers to show more consideration for restaurant staff by giving them plenty of time to prepare the bill.
c restaurants to teach waiters not to disappear just when customers want to pay and go.
d customers to pay their bills in good time.

15

Spotlight on vocabulary: eating and drinking

Answer each question. Then discuss the difference between the words or phrases in italics. Give examples.

1 To wipe your mouth while eating, would you use a *napkin* or a *table-cloth*?
2 Are plates classed as *crockery* or *cutlery*?
3 To boil milk, would you use a *kettle* or a *saucepan*?
4 Is salad usually served in a *bowl* or a *jar*?
5 Do you *slice* or *split* bread?
6 Are onions *cut down* or *chopped*?
7 Do you peel *potatoes* or *peas*?
8 Are eggs *beaten* or *mashed*?
9 Does *jam* or *marmalade* taste sweet?
10 If you are eating food which tastes good, is the food *tasteful* or *tasty*?
11 Is food *swallowed* or *sipped*?
12 In a restaurant, would you ask the waiter for another bread *crumb* or *roll*?
13 Having put some milk and sugar in a cup of coffee, would you stir the coffee with a *teaspoon* or *tablespoon*?
14 Do you *sprinkle* or *spread* butter on bread?
15 If you want roast beef for lunch, is the beef put *in the oven* or *under the grill* for a couple of hours?
16 Can carrots be eaten *raw* or *crude*?
17 In a pub, would you ask for a *pint* or *barrel* of beer?
18 Michael likes white wine, but not if it is sweet. Does he like to drink *dry* or *sour* wine?
19 If you are famished, are you *starving* or *peckish*?
20 If you drink too much alcohol, are you likely to have *indigestion* or a *hangover* the following morning?

Spotlight on phrasal verbs

Using *look* or *make*, complete each sentence with a phrasal verb so that it means exactly the same as the sentence printed above it. You will need to use the following words: *after, down, for, into, off, on, out, over/through, round, to, up* and *with*.

He's seeking work.
He's *looking for work*.

1 Everybody respects him.
Everybody … .

2 She has a low opinion of her neighbours.
She … .

3 I shall investigate the matter.
I shall … .

4 They just watched and did nothing.
They just … .

5 Be careful! There's a car coming towards you.
… .

6 He raised his head and smiled.
He … .

7 He searched for her number in the telephone directory.
He … .

8 She will take care of you when I am gone.
She will … .

9 After viewing the house inside, we decided not to buy it.
After … .

10 When revising, you should study carefully all the exercises in this book.
When revising, you should … .

11 He grabbed my handbag and headed towards the door.
He grabbed my handbag and … .

12 I could just manage to see the road sign through the fog.
I could just … .

13 The thieves escaped with the jewels.
The thieves … .

14 Did you invent that story?
Did you … ?

15 Nothing could compensate for the loss of his parents.
Nothing could … .

Spotlight on completion

Fill each of the numbered blanks in the following passage. Use only one word in each space.

When Peter arrived (1) … the railway station (2) … Paris to catch the train for London, he discovered that he had (3) … his passport back at the hotel (4) … he had stayed the (5) … four days. The train was (6) … to leave in half (7) … hour. If he hurried, he (8) … just have (9) … to return. As he was looking for a taxi at the station entrance, a voice behind him said: 'Do you want a porter, sir?'
'Yes,' Peter replied, 'please look (10) … my luggage. I have a (11) … seat on the two o'clock train for London.' The porter nodded, and said that he (12) … wait for him. (13) … were very many people in the streets at (14) … time of day, and the taxi (15) … longer than Peter had (16) … to get (17) … the hotel. Fortunately, he had no difficulty in (18) … the passport and he (19) … the station five minutes before the (20) … of the train.

Pause for thought

What is the origin of the expression *to take something with a pinch of salt* ?

When we doubt the accuracy of a statement and want to say that we will only accept it with great or certain reservations, we often use such phrases as *I'd take it with a pinch of salt if I were you* or *You should take what he says with a pinch of salt.* It is also possible to say *with a grain of salt.*

For a great many years, salt has been used as both an essential seasoning for animal food, and as a preservative. The origin of this expression lies in these two uses of salt!

We season food with salt in order to make it taste pleasant. In other words, a pinch of salt with something may help you to swallow it. Thus, if somebody's words are hard to swallow, *you should take them with a pinch of salt* !

Salt is also used as a preservative to prevent meat from going off. In other words, salt stops meat from becoming poisonous. In ancient times, people thought that salt contained magical powers precisely because it could preserve meat for such a long time. Accordingly, people started sprinkling salt on food suspected of containing poison, and it soon became customary to eat a questionable dish only with salt.

Thus, if you suspect that there is something wrong with a statement, *you should take it with a pinch of salt.*

15

Spotlight on spelling

Study the words for a minute. Then read out a word to a partner. Ask him or her to spell the word aloud. Check his or her spelling.

accuracy	disguised	guest	requested
alcohol	evaporated	illuminated	saucepan
carrot	exaggerate	pleasant	technique
compass	gesture	pleasure	tomatoes
cutlery	grabbed	psychological	whether

Writing

Write an account of a visit to a restaurant. End with the statement: *I shall definitely not go back to that restaurant!* (120 – 180 words)

Speaking

1 Choose one of the photographs below and comment on it.
2 Do you prefer to have breakfast on your own or in the company of others?
3 Do you prefer to watch television or read a book while having your dinner, or do you prefer your meals at home to be more formal?
4 What do you consider to be good or bad table manners?
5 What do you think of fast food restaurants?

Unit 16

Accuracy building 1

Choose the most appropriate word or phrase to complete each statement. After deciding which is the correct answer, focus your attention on the alternatives. When can they be used?

1 The lorry was … with videos and television sets.
a carrying *b* full *c* loaded *d* transporting

2 Don't be late. The curtain goes up at eight o'clock … .
a dot *b* exact *c* dead *d* sharp

3 Nearly everybody is … to some form of stress.
a affected *b* subject *c* victim *d* under

4 You must … the accident.
a notify *b* inform *c* state *d* report

5 The best speakers are those who are brief and … the point.
a up to *b* over *c* at *d* to

6 I can hear her … in her room. What's upset her this time?
a sobbing *b* giggling *c* growling *d* humming

7 You must watch your speed when driving through a … area.
a pedestrian *b* built-up *c* secluded *d* traffic-free

8 As soon as the lion-tamer … his whip, the lions began jumping through the hoops.
a cast *b* snapped *c* clicked *d* cracked

9 That photograph has brought back such happy … .
a souvenirs *b* remembrances *c* memories *d* memoirs

10 He's wearing a pink shirt, green trousers and white shoes. There's no accounting … taste!
a in *b* for *c* with *d* by

11 There are about 500 apple trees growing in that particular … .
a meadow *b* orchard *c* hamlet *d* well

12 He ran as fast as he could so … not to be late for school.
a that *b* in order *c* for *d* as

13 The joke you've just told me is as old as the … !
a hills *b* pyramids *c* universe *d* stars

14 … is your flat like?
a How *b* Which *c* What *d* Where

15 You're driving too fast. Please slow … .
a up *b* more *c* down *d* now

16 I caught the train by the … of my teeth.
a edge *b* back *c* skin *d* fillings

17 He has served his … and will be released from prison tomorrow.
a punishment *b* imprisonment *c* sentence *d* jail

18 We waited until the storm had blown over ... we set off again.
a before *b* then *c* after *d* when

19 She went to the baker's and bought two ... of bread.
a pieces *b* crusts *c* loaves *d* slices

20 A jury consists of twelve men and women chosen at ... from the list of those entitled to vote.
a chance *b* hazard *c* luck *d* random

21 Hundreds of people in Wales were ... by a mysterious disease last year.
a stricken *b* sickened *c* bitten *d* infested

22 There is no truth ... the story that an ostrich buries its head in the sand when threatened.
a about *b* of *c* in *d* with

23 He ... off while watching television.
a slept *b* snored *c* dozed *d* winked

24 Farmers ... pesticides on their crops to protect them from insects.
a spray *b* grow *c* paint *d* throw

25 The French ... more cheese than any other nation.
a digest *b* absorb *c* consume *d* feed

Accuracy building 2

Now complete the following statements from memory. Do not look back at the previous exercise.

1 The ship was ... with agricultural machinery.
2 Make sure you are here tomorrow at nine o'clock ... !
3 Everyone is ... to the law of the land.
4 You should ... the matter to the proper authorities.
5 He came straight ... the point.
6 I found her ... her heart out.
7 The speed limit is usually 30 mph in a ... area.
8 The moment he ... his whip, the animals started performing their tricks.
9 Do you have happy ... of your childhood?
10 I cannot account ... his present behaviour.
11 We have a lot of pear trees in our ... .
12 She walked quietly into the room so ... not to wake the baby up.
13 Everybody knows that joke. It's as old as the ... .
14 ... was the weather like?
15 He slowed ... as he approached the crossroads.
16 We caught the train by the ... of our teeth.
17 He was found guilty and received a heavy ... .
18 He waited until the following day ... he telephoned her.
19 Could you get me two ... of brown bread?
20 He picked a number at ... .
21 When his wife died, he was ... with grief.
22 There is no truth ... the rumours you have heard.
23 He ... off while reading a book in his favourite armchair.
24 Why don't you ... this on your hair?
25 Cars ... petrol.

16

Spotlight on description

Finish each sentence in such a way that it means exactly the same as the sentence above it.

Her son is a boy with fair hair.
Her son is *a fair-haired boy*.

1 Her hair reaches down to her shoulders.
She has … .

2 He has broad shoulders.
He is … .

3 He is in his fifties.
He is … .

4 She is about thirty-eight years old.
She is in … .

5 My daughter is ten years old.
I have a … .

6 Her heart is broken.
She is … .

7 He is neither very tall nor very short.
He is of … .

8 She is neither stupid nor brilliant.
She is of … .

9 He is a tallish man.
He is a … .

10 Her face has been tanned by the sun.
Her face is … .

11 He was wearing a woollen sweater. It was brown and it was old.
He was wearing … .

12 Her hair is blonde. It is wavy and it is long.
She has … .

13 Her eyes are round. They are large and they are blue.
She has … .

14 The flight lasted eight hours.
It was an … .

15 The course lasts three months.
It is a … .

16 The journey took two days.
It was a … .

17 That man near the door looks suspicious.
There's a … .

18 His eyes looked sad.
He had … .

Have a laugh

Lady Agatha Hawkins, being a woman with a title, was often invited to formal dinners where people were seated according to their rank and status.

One evening she was invited to a dinner given by the deputy Prime Minister.

There were about one hundred guests and when they had all sat down to dinner, Lady Agatha noticed that, according to the strict rule of precedence, she had been placed too far down the table.

Being an arrogant woman, she felt most upset and complained bitterly to the nearest attendant. Hasty enquiries confirmed that she should in fact have been seated next to the deputy Prime Minister himself, and so everyone on her side of the table was asked to stand up and change places.

As soon as she was seated in what she considered to be her rightful place, Lady Agatha tried to make light of the trouble she had caused.

'I imagine that you and your wife must find these questions of precedence very tiresome, sir,' she said to the deputy Prime Minister.

'Not really,' he answered. 'Experience has taught us that those who matter don't mind, and those who mind don't matter.'

19 He dressed very smartly for the occasion.
He was … .

20 The child behaves very badly.
He is a … .

Spotlight on *say* or *tell*

Complete each sentence with the correct form of *say* or *tell*.

1 You should … what you mean.
2 Who … you that? Was it Susan?
3 Who … that? Was it Mike?
4 I've got something important to … to you.
5 It is … that he is a very generous man.
6 He's very good at … jokes.
7 I was … to mind my own business.
8 She … she would see him later.
9 … her to hurry up.
10 She is … to be an alcoholic.
11 It's wrong to … a lie.
12 I can't … you how sorry I am.
13 He kept … how sorry he was.
14 Would you like me to … you a story?
15 They look the same to me. I can't … one from the other.

Reading

Read the passage below. Following the passage, you will find five unfinished statements. Decide which of the alternatives, *a*, *b*, *c* or *d*, best completes each statement.

MOTORWAY MADNESS

Dodgem drivers and eccentrics are causing chaos on Europe's most overcrowded motorway, say M25 traffic police.

Exasperated patrolmen have nicknamed the chaotic London ring road Death Race 2000. They say that some drivers seem to be overtaken by madness – while admitting that occasionally the results are bizarrely comic.

Officers still tell of the madcap motor-cyclist who tried to compete with speeding BMWs and juggernauts near St Albans, Hertfordshire. Jake Mangle-Wurzel, the self-proclaimed *King of the Eccentrics*, had his dog riding in a basket on the back of the bike. A fan on the front of the machine was a *pedestrian repellent*, he said. A metal pole and amber builder's light formed a makeshift lightning conductor to protect him if a storm blew up. And a washing line strung across the top of the bike, he told stunned policemen, was to dry his underwear.

Jake, 52, denied driving a dangerous vehicle and the case was laughed out of court by magistrates.

But there are plenty of other M25 users who drive police to distraction. On another day, they spotted two joggers trying to run round the 117-mile hard shoulder for charity. The runners were finally persuaded to attempt their marathon on less dangerous ground.

Eccentric bird fancier Sean Edmeads decided that he didn't need to phone for help when his van broke down. Instead, he sent two of his racing pigeons winging off to the family home near Sevenoaks, Kent, to fetch his father. Dad, alerted by a message attached to the birds, arrived by car at the same time as traffic police.

Officers once had to rescue an elderly woman driver who suddenly had an attack of motorway nerves at the crowded junction of the M4 and M25. She abandoned her car and fled to the nearest SOS phone screaming for help. Police took her off for a calming cup of tea and moved her car to a quieter road.

In other incidents, police have seen businessmen cruising at 90 mph chatting away on their car phones and holding the wheel with only one hand. Other drivers have tried to drive backwards down blocked-up slip roads. And some motorists have allowed their children to play on the carriage-way during long jams.

Sadly, the M25 madness causes tragedy too. Four people were burned alive last October when a car crashed while trying to do a U-turn. And more than fifty people have been killed and 1500 injured in six years.

'People drive as if there is no tomorrow – and for some that becomes true,' said one policeman.

(From an article in the *Daily Express*)

1 The M25
a passes through London.
b goes right round London.
c passes London on one side only.
d runs around in circles.

2 Jake Mangle-Wurzel's motorbike
a has a device on the front to scare off pedestrians.
b was found not guilty of being a dangerous vehicle.
c is designed in such a way that it provides shelter for Jake during a storm.
d has a washing line tied across the handle-bars.

3 It would seem that the police
a enjoy patrolling the M25 because a lot of funny things happen.
b think that jogging for charity is a dangerous sport that should not be encouraged.
c consider the M25 to be dangerously overcrowded with dodgem drivers and eccentrics.
d are becoming fed up with the growing number of thoughtless motorists who put others in danger.

4 According to the passage,
a some motorists stop to let their children play on the motorway during long journeys.
b a middle-aged woman driver lost her nerve and abandoned her car just where one motorway joins another.
c some drivers have tried to drive backwards down slippery roads blocked with traffic.
d two pigeons conveyed an SOS message to the father of a motorist who was stuck on the M25.

5 According to the police,
a many motorists drive like maniacs on the M25.
b many drivers on the M25 seem to believe that it is better to arrive late than never.
c many motorists are driven crazy by the thought of driving on the M25.
d many drivers seem to believe that it is better to be safe than sorry.

16

Spotlight on vocabulary: motoring

Answer each question. Then discuss the difference between the words or phrases in italics. Give examples.

1 Do you run *into* or *out of* petrol?
2 Do you get *on* or *into* a car?
3 If your car runs into the back of another vehicle, is your front bumper likely to be *dented* or *smashed*?
4 Do cars *skate* or *skid* on a slippery road surface?
5 Peter wants a lift in your car but you can't fit him in. Would you tell Peter that there is no *space* or *room* for him in the car?
6 Do cars *swerve* or *do a somersault* to avoid hitting something in front of them?
7 Does a *roundabout* or a *bypass* make it possible for a motorist to avoid driving through a town?
8 Would a sign tell you there is a *deviation* or a *diversion* ahead?
9 If there is no air in one of your tyres, have you got a *flat* or *puncture* tyre?
10 Do you look *in* or *at* the mirror when you want to see if there is any traffic behind you?
11 Do you need a *licence* or a *permit* to drive a car?
12 Is luggage placed in the *boot* or *bonnet* of a car?
13 If you want to use a petrol pump at a service station and you need some assistance, will an *attendant* or an *assistant* give you a hand?
14 Are the lights on the front of a car called the *head* or *rear* lights?
15 To accelerate or slow down, do you change *gear* or *the speedometer*?
16 Does a motorway have *lanes* or *tracks*?
17 During the rush hour, is the traffic *heavy* or *strong*?
18 Is the special area where you can park your car called a *car park* or *parking*?
19 If your car hits a lorry, have you *collided with* or *run over* the lorry?
20 Are you taught to drive by a driving *tutor* or *instructor*?

Spotlight on phrasal verbs

Using *put* or *run*, complete each sentence with a phrasal verb so that it means exactly the same as the sentence printed above it. You will need to use the following words: *after, aside, away, back, down, for, forward, from, in, into, off, on, out, up* and *with*.

He did an extra hour's work.
He *put in an extra hour's work.*

1 He has gained weight.
He … .

2 Can you give me a bed for the night?
Can you … ?

3 The concert has been postponed until next week.
The concert … .

4 They extinguished the fire.
They … .

5 She won't tolerate bad manners.
She won't … .

6 The old dog was in such pain that there was no alternative but to have it killed.
The old dog was in such pain that there was no alternative but to … .

7 The awful smell from the kitchen made me lose interest in my food.
The awful smell from the kitchen … .

8 They have raised their prices for the third time this year.
They … .

9 I am saving some money for a rainy day.
I am … .

10 He pretended to have a French accent.
He … .

11 They pursued the thief.
They … .

12 He looks weak and exhausted.
He looks … .

13 I met Jane by chance in the High Street this morning.
I … .

14 The team from Halifax won the competition really easily.
The team from Halifax … .

15 Eight children have escaped from that orphanage in the past year.
Eight children have … .

Spotlight on completion

Fill each of the numbered blanks in the following passage. Use only one word in each space.

There was once a tailor who was an ill-tempered man. His wife was a good, industrious woman but he (1) … often beat her for no reason (2) … all.
When the magistrates discovered (3) … badly he treated his wife, they had him brought to court and (4) … him to a term of imprisonment. He lived (5) … bread and water for some weeks, and then was (6) … out after he had been made to swear he would not beat his wife any more and that he would live with her peaceably 'for better or for worse' (7) … all married couples should.
For a time things went smoothly, but the husband soon went back to his old (8) … . He became quarrelsome, and because he was not (9) … to beat his wife he caught her by the hair and shook her. The wife escaped into the garden, but he ran (10) … her and chased her round and round. Anything that came handy (sticks, stones and so on), he picked up and hurled (11) … her. If he (12) … her he laughed, if he missed, he jumped up and down howling (13) … a madman. He went on (14) … this manner for so

Pause for thought

What is the origin of *lunatic*, and why does *head over heels in love* mean *madly in love*?

A *lunatic* is an insane person. The word comes from the Latin *lunaticus*, which means *a person affected by the moon.* The Romans believed that the mind was affected by the moon, and that the greater the moonlight, the greater the intensity of madness caused. Accordingly, mentally ill people were supposed to be at their worst when the moon was full.

Head over heels is in fact a meaningless phrase, since it's impossible to get your head over your heels! Originally, the phrase was *heels over head.* During the Middle Ages, hundreds of crimes carried the death penalty. Two types of hangings were widely practised: a man sentenced to die was hanged by the neck until dead; and a man merely given a strong warning was sentenced to *hang by the heels.* The expression *heels over head* came into use to indicate a state of helplessness or confusion (when your world has been turned upside-down).

Eventually the practice of hanging by the heels was stopped. People forgot the grim meaning of *heels over head* and changed the phrase to *head over heels.*

We can use *head over heels* to describe someone doing a somersault, or to describe that intense feeling of helplessness experienced by people who fall in love.

long that at last the neighbours felt bound to interfere and come to the wife's rescue. The tailor was again brought up before the magistrates and reminded (15) ... his promise to keep the peace.
'Gentlemen,' he answered, 'I have (16) ... my word. I haven't beaten her, and I have shared things for better and for worse with her.'
'How is that possible,' inquired one of the judges, 'when such serious charges are brought against you?'
'I did not beat her, gentlemen. I was (17) ... going to comb her hair with my hand when she ran off into the garden. I followed her to remind her of her duties, and to emphasise my words I may (18) ... taken the first thing that came to hand to throw at her. Whenever I hit her it was better for me and worse for her, and whenever I missed it was better for her and worse for me. So, you see, we shared everything equally.'
The judges were not satisfied (19) ... this answer and (20) ... him back to prison.

Spotlight on spelling

Study the words for a minute. Then read out a word to a partner. Ask him or her to spell the word aloud. Check his or her spelling.

agricultural
attached
bitterly
chatting
enquiries
experience
giggling
helplessness
industrious
interfere
memories
orphanage
postponed
quieter
slippery
nickname
sobbing
stricken
tiresome
weight

16

Writing

You were involved in a car accident last week. Write a letter to a friend describing what happened. (120 – 180 words)

Speaking

Comment on the photographs on this and the next page. Compare and contrast the different images presented.

16

Unit 17

Accuracy building 1

1 Choose the most appropriate word or phrase to complete each statement. After deciding which is the correct answer, focus your attention on the alternatives. When can they be used?

1 The train … up at the station.
a halted *b* paused *c* pulled *d* ceased

2 His behaviour has … a great deal of anger and resentment among his colleagues.
a arisen *b* aroused *c* raised *d* risen

3 Farmers work from dawn to … .
a dusk *b* dark *c* sunrise *d* daybreak

4 You'd better ring the airport to … the flight.
a guarantee *b* ensure *c* control *d* confirm

5 We must expect the worst. The surgeon who operated on him has said that he might not pull … .
a off *b* through *c* in *d* over

6 You can count … me. I won't let you down.
a of *b* with *c* in *d* on

7 He gave her a friendly … , but she ignored him completely.
a blink *b* wink *c* flicker *d* snarl

8 I'm … . I have spent all my money.
a short *b* run out *c* broke *d* over

9 They were taken to hospital and treated … shock.
a by *b* for *c* against *d* to

10 She … when he told her he loved her.
a blushed *b* grunted *c* howled *d* yelled

11 I intend to … up my own business.
a establish *b* promote *c* set *d* launch

12 Please wipe your feet on the door … .
a rug *b* tapestry *c* carpet *d* mat

13 We haven't got a garage, but you can park your car in the … .
a drive *b* kerb *c* pavement *d* gutter

14 She'll be back … .
a shortly *b* a while *c* at present *d* finally

15 How do you … your new job?
a discover *b* get *c* find *d* obtain

16 The worst part of dental treatment is when the dentist uses his … on your teeth.
a screwdriver *b* drill *c* spade *d* spanner

17 My hand has gone … . I can't feel a thing.
a senseless *b* unfeeling *c* insensitive *d* numb

18 There is no trace of the ship. It must have … to the bottom of the sea.
a sink *b* sank *c* sunk *d* sunken

19 His behaviour leaves a lot to be … .
a wanted *b* desired *c* needed *d* wished

20 My wife became ill during the night and I had to send … a doctor.
a off *b* out *c* for *d* round

21 She … him across the face.
a punched *b* slapped *c* thumped *d* patted

22 A woodpecker uses its … to peck at wood.
a nose *b* head *c* beak *d* feathers

23 With its huge jaws open, the alligator … along the river bank towards the unsuspecting child.
a crawled *b* hopped *c* galloped *d* skipped

24 My … husband was known for his kindness and gentleness. Everybody misses him.
a recent *b* late *c* past *d* latest

25 The sound gradually … away.
a fainted *b* disappeared *c* evaporated *d* died

Accuracy building 2

Now complete the following statements from memory. Do not look back at the previous exercise.

1 The lorry … up at the service station.
2 The project has … a great deal of interest.
3 Farmers plough their fields from dawn to … .
4 Please … in writing what you told us over the phone.
5 Despite his severe injuries and three major operations, he somehow managed to pull … .
6 I know I can count … you.
7 Henry! Why did you … at that woman? Who is she?
8 He's always … . What does he do with his money?
9 He's being treated … cancer.
10 She … when he gave her a bunch of roses in front of all the office staff.
11 He's going to … up his own company.
12 He wiped his feet on the door … .
13 He parked his car in the … .
14 They'll be back … .
15 How do you … your new flat?
16 He used a … to make a hole in the wall.
17 Her fingers were … with cold.
18 The boat must have hit a rock and … to the bottom of the sea.
19 Your work leaves a lot to be … .
20 Have you sent … a doctor?
21 Before I could apologise, she … me across the face.
22 A bird uses its … to peck at food.
23 She stood dumbstruck with terror as the tarantula … up her arm.
24 Her … husband was an unpleasant fellow. Everybody disliked him.
25 We heard a low murmur that gradually … away.

17

Spotlight on some useful grammar points

Finish each of the following sentences in such a way that it means exactly the same as the sentence printed above it.

Andrew is to blame.
It's *Andrew's fault.*

1 They live in a cottage at the top of a steep hill.
The cottage ... .

2 She works in a restaurant opposite the police station.
The restaurant ... .

3 You don't have to shout!
There's ... .

4 How much did the car cost?
How much did you ... ?

5 How did the fire start?
What was ... ?

6 How do you earn your living?
What do ... ?

7 Whose camera is this?
Who ... ?

8 Andrew lent Mark fifty pounds last week.
Mark ... .

9 I was introduced to a man with friends in high places.
The man ... .

10 There's nothing left to eat.
There isn't ... .

11 There isn't any milk in the fridge.
There's ... .

12 He was friendly when he spoke to me.
He spoke to me ... .

13 It wasn't easy to concentrate.
I found ... .

14 I wrote her a letter, but I haven't received a reply.
I haven't ... .

15 Generally speaking, I am pleased with the progress he is making.
On ... .

Have a laugh

'Has Matthew got long to live?' Robert asked the hospital doctor.
'I'm afraid not. He could die at any moment.'
On hearing the bad news, Robert went immediately to see Matthew, his friend and business partner.
Matthew was lying in bed and he was so weak that he could hardly speak. When he saw Robert sitting beside him, he raised his head from the pillow and began to whisper.
'Robert ... Robert ... '
'Rest, Matthew, rest,' Robert advised. 'Save your strength.'
'No,' insisted the dying man. 'I can't. I must clear my conscience before I die. I have been a very bad partner, Robert. And I've been a disloyal friend. I was the one who stole the £50,000 from the office safe. I was the one who reported you to the tax inspector. I was the one who told your wife about you and the secretary. I was the one who ... '
'Don't worry, Matthew,' said Robert gently. 'Please don't worry. I was the one who put poison in your cup of tea.'

17

Reading

Read the passage below. Following the passage, you will find five unfinished statements. Decide which of the alternatives, *a*, *b*, *c* or *d*, best completes each statement.

HEAVY WEATHER

Countless roads, including motorways, became impassable when Arctic blizzards swept most of Britain yesterday, bringing total chaos.

Last night, many of those who had set out on what should have been routine journeys were still trapped in their vehicles, fighting off the cold as rescue teams battled to get through.

Helicopters airlifted sixty stranded people to safety from the snowbound A66 last night. Throughout Britain snow-ploughs were being used to unblock roads which had left whole towns and villages cut off. A pensioner collapsed and died as ambulancemen battled to get through to a cut-off village. A paramedic was flown in by helicopter to Highworth, near Swindon, but the man was already dead.

In Oxfordshire a pregnant woman who was about to go into labour became trapped in her car near the village of Enstone. Police contacted a midwife and set out to save the distraught mother-to-be, only to find themselves trapped by huge drifts. Finally a rescue convoy fought its way through.

Four youths, trapped in their car on a snowbound Pennine road, saved themselves with the help of a mobile telephone. They spent the night huddled in their car on the A537 Macclesfield-Buxton road, trying to contact police but constantly being defeated by interference. Eventually they decided to risk making their way through the heavy snow. Scrambling out of the car and through the drifts, they managed to find shelter in a derelict farm building. After finally getting through to the police, they were winched to safety by a RAF helicopter.

The sudden attack of Britain's worst winter weather for years stretched emergency services and contingency plans to the limit.

Hospitals, many running on their own generators because of widespread power cuts, put out radio appeals in some areas for doctors and nurses. They dealt with case after case of exposure affecting people who had been forced to abandon their vehicles.

At Banbury, one of three Oxfordshire towns cut off, police set up an emergency incident room. Throughout the day all seven lines were flooded with calls from trapped drivers – and from people anxious over the fate of relatives and friends.

Hundreds of thousands of homes were hit by power cuts. Water authorities in the Severn Valley issued warnings to conserve supplies after water treatment centres were affected by electricity cuts.

A snow-making machine, which Rochester City Council had hired two months ago at a cost of several thousand pounds, was made redundant with the arrival of real snow. The machine had been hired to add authenticity to a Dickensian Christmas festival organised by the council. Instead they got more than enough of the real thing!

(from a report in the *Sunday Express*)

1 According to the passage, most parts of Britain were affected by
a a spell of mild weather.
b heavy snow storms.
c icy winds and torrential rain.
d fog and ice on the roads.

2 Conditions were so bad that
a some rescuers had to be rescued themselves.
b helicopters had to be used to unblock some roads.
c several elderly people collapsed and died before help could reach them.
d there was no access whatsoever to whole towns and villages.

3 Four youths
a abandoned their car and took shelter in a disused farm building, where they were eventually found by the police.
b used a carphone to summon help when they found themselves stranded in the snow.
c risked their lives to reach a farm building where they found help.
d failed to contact the police on their mobile telephone because of the adverse weather conditions.

4 Because of widespread power cuts,
a hundreds of thousands of homes were without water.
b hospitals in some areas put out radio appeals for doctors and nurses.
c many towns and villages were cut off.
d many hospitals had to fall back on their own means of generating electricity.

5 It is clear from the passage that
a Rochester City Council did not anticipate a white Christmas.
b the present snow storms will save Rochester City Council a lot of money.
c such atrocious winter weather is normal in Britain.
d Britain is totally prepared for a sudden attack of very bad weather.

Spotlight on vocabulary: the weather

Answer each question. Then discuss the difference between the words or phrases in italics. Give examples.

1 You have gone for a stroll and it has started to rain. Are you walking *in* or *under* the rain?
2 If it rains for just a few minutes, do we refer to that rainfall as a *drop* or a *shower*?
3 If it is raining very heavily, is the rain *pouring down* or is it *pouring rain*?
4 Should a raincoat be *watertight* or *waterproof*?
5 Does it rain *cats and dogs* or *buckets and mops*?
6 Do we save up for a *rainy* or *raining* day?
7 Are *droughts* or *draughts* the consequence of too little rain?
8 If it is slightly cold, is it *chilly* or *freezing*?
9 Do we describe a very hard winter as *strict* or *severe*?
10 Is a light, refreshing wind called a *gust* or a *breeze*?
11 Does the weather *twist* or *turn* cold at night?
12 If you are feeling slightly unwell, are you feeling *a bit under the weather* or *under a cloud*?
13 If the weather has turned cold and is expected to last for some time, has the cold weather *set in* or *settled down?*
14 If you have just enjoyed a few days of pleasant weather, have you enjoyed a *term* or *spell* of good weather?
15 Which is thinner, *mist* or *fog*?
16 Which is harder, *hail* or *haze*?
17 Do meteorologists *foretell* or *forecast* the weather?
18 Would you expect to find *frost* or *icebergs* on the ground in early winter?
19 Can a tree be struck by *lightning* or *thunder*?
20 When a great fuss is being made over nothing, do we say it is *a storm in a teacup* or *just a drop in the ocean*?

17

Spotlight on singular and plural

Choose the correct alternative in each of the following sentences.

1 Most of the rubbish ... collected this morning.
a was *b* were

2 The information you gave me ... inaccurate.
a was *b* were

3 All the furniture in this room ... antique.
a is *b* are

4 The police ... looking for two men in connection with the robbery.
a is *b* are

5 The news of his resignation ... shocked us all.
a has *b* have

6 My luggage ... missing.
a is *b* are

7 These trousers ... fit me.
a doesn't *b* don't

8 Why don't you use ... scissors?
a this *b* these

9 £10,000 ... a lot of money.
a is *b* are

10 Everybody ... glad to see him again.
a was *b* were

11 England ... playing Wales at Wembley this afternoon.
a is *b* are

12 One of my ... is married.
a brother *b* brothers

13 One of the tyres ... a puncture.
a has *b* have

14 Neither John nor Peter ... willing to help.
a is *b* are

15 Two ... eggs, please.
a dozen *b* dozens

16 We plan to stay for ... five days.
a another *b* other

17 Don't forget to buy some ... .
a fruit *b* fruits

18 I don't usually mind walking, but ten miles ... a long way!
a is *b* are

19 Could you lend me a ... pounds?
a hundred *b* hundreds

20 Cycling is a ... of transport.
a mean *b* means

Spotlight on phrasal verbs

Using *take* or *turn*, complete each sentence with a phrasal verb so that it means exactly the same as the sentence printed above it. You will need to use the following words: *after, away, down, in, on, out, over, to* and *up*.

The aircraft left the ground.
The aircraft *took off*.

1 I didn't like him at first, but now we are the best of friends.
I didn't … .

2 We employ extra staff during the summer season.
We … .

3 Why don't you dedicate some time to a hobby or a sport?
Why … ?

4 I was fooled by his smart appearance and gentle voice. I didn't find out until later that he was a criminal.
I was … .

5 A larger company has taken control of our firm.
Our firm … .

6 He has the same temperament as his father.
He … .

7 Anything you say will be recorded in writing and may be used against you in court.
Anything you say will … .

8 I'm tired. I think I'll go to bed.
I'm tired. I think I'll … .

9 We've decided to reject their offer.
We've decided to … .

10 The restaurant was full, so we were not allowed to enter.
The restaurant was full, so we were … .

11 He arrived just as we were about to leave.
He … .

12 How was the party in the end? Was it a success?
How did … ?

Spotlight on completion

Fill each of the numbered blanks in the following passage. Use only one word in each space.

There was once a farmer who lived near Mallow. From sunrise to (1) … he toiled (2) … his farm. His wife did what she (3) … to help him, as their children were too young to work (4) … the fields.
The poor woman (5) … after the house, milked the cow, boiled the potatoes, and carried the eggs to market. (6) … the end of the summer, they had always saved (7) … money to pay the rent.
At last came a bad year. Day (8) … day the rain (9) … down. Their small crop of oats was spoiled, the chickens died and the pigs fell (10) … . When the rent was due, there was (11) … money to pay the landlord.
'What can we do, Molly?' said the farmer sadly to his wife.

17

'You must take the cow to Cork, Mick, and sell her,' said Molly. 'Monday is market day, (12) ... you must go tomorrow.'
'And what (13) ... we do when she is gone?' he asked, not very willing to part (14) ... the cow.
'Och! Now you are looking for trouble (15) ... it meets you.'
'I believe you are right, Molly. I will go tomorrow; and now you must put a needle and thread through my coat, for it is torn under the arm.'
Early (16) ... morning, he took his stick in his hand and drove his cow slowly (17) ... the road. It was a fine day and the sun (18) ... brightly on the fields. After six long miles the farmer came to the bottom of a hill: Bottle Hill it is (19) ... now, but that (20) ... not the name of it then.

Spotlight on spelling

Study the words for a minute. Then read out a word to a partner. Ask him or her to spell the word aloud. Check his or her spelling.

access
adverse
antique
atrocious
blizzard
dumbstruck
electricity
emergency
eventually
guarantee
impassable
murmur
pillow
potatoes
rubbish
scissors
torrential
traditional
unpleasant
whisper

Pause for thought

What is the origin of the expression *to rain cats and dogs*?

The origin of this expression lies in the traditional stories or legends of northern Europe. In northern mythology the cat is supposed to have great influence on the weather, and the dog (said to be one of the attendants of Odin, the storm god) always announces the coming of wind.

Thus we use the combination of *cats and dogs* to describe a heavy downpour of rain, because cats symbolise the downpouring rain and dogs symbolise the strong gusts of wind accompanying a rainstorm.

Writing

You went on holiday for a week and it rained every day of the holiday. Write a letter to a friend describing what you did during that week. (120 – 180 words)

Speaking

1 What is the person in the photograph on the next page doing?
2 What do you think might happen if it suddenly started to snow heavily?
3 Are you keen on any winter sport? Which one(s)?
4 Does the weather ever get you down? What sort of weather do you prefer?
5 Which is your favourite season of the year? Why?

17

Key

Unit 1

Accuracy building 1

1 b 2 c 3 a 4 b 5 d 6 c 7 d 8 a 9 c 10 a 11 b
12 c 13 d 14 c 15 b 16 d 17 d 18 b 19 c 20 c 21 c
22 c 23 a 24 b 25 c

Accuracy building 2

1 at 2 get 3 down 4 stand 5 spent 6 struck 7 Congratulations
8 top 9 during 10 damaged 11 stroll 12 up 13 resort 14 Shoplifters
15 strike 16 enrol 17 fox 18 looks as if 19 hoovering 20 since
21 pick 22 ever 23 course 24 identical 25 otherwise

Spotlight on comparatives and superlatives

1 heavier 2 more heavily 3 easiest 4 worse 5 thinner 6 the largest
7 more quietly 8 the most exciting 9 more depressed 10 healthier

1 I don't think Michael is as good-looking as Tony.
2 Sue is prettier than Ann.
3 It is much / far hotter in Africa than in England.
4 Peter is a much worse tennis-player than I am.
5 He drives (even) more slowly than she does.
6 The old machine works much less efficiently than the new one.
7 The second car is four times as expensive as the first one / car.
8 Model A is not nearly as expensive as Model B.
9 France is three times as large / big as England.
10 There were fewer people than I had expected.
11 I earn less money than you (do).
12 The film they made is not as good as the novel he wrote.
13 This one is the same as that one.
14 The harder you work, the more money you will earn.
15 It's getting more and more difficult to buy a house in London.
16 That is / was the most boring film I have ever seen.
17 Alan earns the most, and Paul earns the least.
18 John is my youngest son and Mark is my / the eldest (son).
19 Graham is the laziest student / pupil in the class.
20 Margaret is the best tennis-player in the school.

Reading: *Killer blaze*

1 c 2 b 3 c 4 a 5 b

Spotlight on vocabulary: fire

1 helmet 2 hose 3 axe 4 ladder 5 fire extinguisher 6 fire escape
7 fire drill 8 fire-resistant 9 burst into flames 10 on fire 11 set light to it
12 go out

Spotlight on vocabulary: the police

1 police station 2 cell 3 handcuffs 4 siren 5 statement 6 truncheon
7 pursued 8 look into

Key

Spotlight on prepositions

1 in   2 at   3 on   4 in   5 on   6 at   7 in   8 on   9 on   10 at
11 in   12 at   13 in   14 in   15 at

Spotlight on verbs

A I *am* sorry I *am* late. I *missed* my train. *Have* you *been waiting* long?
B About half-an-hour.
A Sorry!
B Never mind.
A *Has* the film already *started*?
B Yes, it *started* twenty minutes ago. *Do* you still *want to go* in?
A No, I *don't think* so. Why *don't* we *go* for a drink instead?
B All right. By the way, *have* you *seen* Peter lately?
A No, I *haven't seen* him for over a month. Why?
B He *owes* me £100. I *lent* him the money three weeks ago, and he *said* he *would pay* me back within a week. But he *seems to have disappeared*!

Unit 2

Accuracy building 1

1 d   2 c   3 b   4 a   5 b   6 c   7 d   8 b   9 b   10 c   11 a
12 b   13 d   14 c   15 b   16 c   17 b   18 c   19 d   20 c   21 b
22 c   23 c   24 d   25 d

Accuracy building 2

1 on   2 had   3 pouring   4 off   5 would   6 by   7 alike   8 to be
9 gold   10 off   11 brakes   12 off   13 frowned   14 had   15 Beware
16 out of   17 could   18 fewer   19 fastest   20 lean   21 veil   22 fancy
23 Whose   24 from continuing   25 racked

Spotlight on the passive

1 Mr Brown is respected by all the staff.
2 Our customers are treated with respect.
3 The air is being polluted by chemicals.
4 The meeting will be held this afternoon in Room 5.
5 The meat should be left in the oven for one hour.
6 The missing documents were found in his coat pocket.
7 You were seen near the scene of the crime.
8 The ship was being unloaded when the fire was discovered.
9 I have never been spoken to like that before!
10 A new bridge has been built over the river.
11 I don't like being told what to do.
12 The work should have been done yesterday.
13 It must have been repaired last week.
14 He is known to be a thief.
15 It is believed (that) he is hiding somewhere in Peru.
16 He is said to have kept all his money hidden under a mattress.
17 The vacuum cleaner needs repairing.
18 I shall have it mended tomorrow.
19 Have you had your hair cut?
20 He was made to work an extra shift.

Key

Reading: *Tickets please*

1 d 2 b 3 c 4 a 5 c

Spotlight on irregular verbs

become	became	become
begin	began	begun
bend	bent	bent
bite	bit	bitten
blow	blew	blown
break	broke	broken
bring	brought	brought
build	built	built
burn	burnt/burned	burnt/burned
buy	bought	bought
catch	caught	caught
choose	chose	chosen
come	came	come
cost	cost	cost
cut	cut	cut
dig	dug	dug
do	did	done
draw	drew	drawn
dream	dreamt/dreamed	dreamt/dreamed
drive	drove	driven
fall	fell	fallen
feed	fed	fed
feel	felt	felt
find	found	found
fight	fought	fought
fly	flew	flown
forget	forgot	forgotten
freeze	froze	frozen
get	got	got
give	gave	given

Spotlight on vocabulary: travelling by train

1 railway timetable 2 lost property office 3 on a luggage rack 4 passengers 5 buffet car 6 level crossing 7 track 8 locomotive 9 signals 10 punch 11 set out on 12 make 13 board 14 change 15 over a loudspeaker

Spotlight on prepositions

1 on, of 2 in 3 in 4 on 5 on 6 of 7 in 8 on, .of 9 of 10 of 11 off 12 in, of 13 in 14 in 15 off

Spotlight on verbs

A *Have* you *typed out* the report yet?
B Yes, here you *are.*
A Thanks.
B Er, *would* it *be* all right if I *went* home early today? My car *needs servicing / to be serviced* and my local garage *shuts* at five.
A This *is* the third time this week that you *have asked* for time off work. On Monday you *said* that your cat *was* ill and that you *had to take* it to the vet before five o'clock. On Tuesday you *asked* me if you *could go* home early because you *were not feeling / didn't feel*

well, and now today you *are asking* me *to let* you *leave* early! What *is* / *'s* more, you only *started* this job last week! *Is* it really necessary *to have* your car *serviced*? *Can't* / *Couldn't* it *be done* at the weekend?

B I *am going* away this weekend. I *don't suppose* I *could leave* work early on Friday afternoon, *could* I?

Unit 3

Accuracy building 1

1 b 2 d 3 b 4 c 5 d 6 d 7 a 8 b 9 d 10 a 11 d
12 c 13 b 14 d 15 a 16 b 17 c 18 c 19 b 20 d 21 b 22 a
23 c 24 a 25 c

Accuracy building 2

1 in 2 saw 3 had 4 suffer 5 as 6 wagging 7 unable 8 some
9 fist 10 get 11 fond 12 tiles 13 provided 14 bunch 15 trip
16 up 17 sore 18 bee 19 desert 20 obstinate 21 put 22 graduating
23 would 24 sheep 25 fed

Spotlight on reported speech

1 She said (that) she was going to Spain the following week.
2 She told Paul she would see him the following / the next day.
3 She told her mother not to wait up for her as she would be home very late.
4 He said (that) they had never been to Italy, but they hoped to go there one day.
5 He told Julie he might see her that evening / night.
6 He complained that it was raining and that someone had taken his umbrella.
7 They invited us to spend the following weekend with them on their yacht.
8 She reminded me to ring her the following Tuesday.
9 She asked us not to smoke in there.
10 He admitted that he had forgotten to order some spare parts.
11 He reminded her that he had given it to her the week before / the previous week.
12 He said (that) he had to finish the report as soon as possible.
13 He advised me to sell the car.
14 She suggested going / (that) we went to Wales that weekend.
15 He suggested (that) I gave / I should give Mary a ring.
16 She asked John what he did for a living.
17 She asked if everything was all right.
18 He asked me if I lived in a flat.
19 He asked Henry why he had stolen the money.
20 I asked the shopkeeper how much the red apples were.

Spotlight on irregular verbs

hear	heard	heard
hide	hid	hidden
hurt	hurt	hurt
keep	kept	kept
know	knew	known
lay	laid	laid
lie	lay	lain
mean	meant	meant
ride	rode	ridden
ring	rang	rung
shake	shook	shaken

shine	shone	shone
shoot	shot	shot
sing	sang	sung
sleep	slept	slept
slide	slid	slid
steal	stole	stolen
stand	stood	stood
tear	tore	torn
win	won	won

Reading: *Wealthy and wise*

1 a 2 b 3 d 4 c 5 d

Spotlight on vocabulary: money

1 pocket money 2 purse 3 income tax 4 wisely 5 overdrawn
6 hard-up 7 reluctant 8 broke 9 as poor as a church mouse 10 banknote
11 borrowed 12 settle 13 cash 14 make out 15 grant 16 pay rise
17 bankrupt 18 pay off 19 worth a great deal of money 20 expenses are paid

Spotlight on prepositions

1 On 2 in 3 on 4 in 5 on 6 on 7 to 8 in 9 at, in 10 to, in
11 To, to 12 at 13 at 14 at 15 in

Spotlight on verbs

A *Have you heard* the news?
B News? What news?
A Andrew *has been promoted* to assistant manager.
B You *are joking*! When *did all this happen*?
A Just this morning. The managing director *came* into our office at about 9.30 and *asked to see* him. Twenty minutes later Andrew *came* back with a huge grin on his face.
B It *makes* you sick, *doesn't* it! How long *has* Andrew *been* with this company? Six months?
A A bit longer. He *arrived* about the same time as Anne *did*.
B Well, I *have been* with this company since I *left* school over five years ago.
A Yes, but you *aren't* / *are not* married to the managing director's daughter!

Unit 4

Accuracy building 1

1 d 2 a 3 c 4 c 5 b 6 a 7 b 8 d 9 d 10 a 11 c 12 b
13 a 14 b 15 d 16 b 17 a 18 c 19 a 20 c 21 b 22 c 23 c 24 b 25 c

Accuracy building 2

1 afraid 2 yours 3 fleet 4 well 5 claws 6 despite 7 endanger 8 run
9 sense 10 fact 11 leaf 12 down 13 steep 14 course 15 discoveries
16 check-up 17 dating 18 believed 19 tan 20 breeds 21 from
22 raise 23 not smoking 24 orphan 25 driving

Spotlight on conditionals

1 I shall be very angry if you are not back by eleven o'clock.
2 If you don't leave straight away, you'll be late for your appointment.
3 Unless we receive the goods by Friday, we shall cancel the order.
4 I won't do it unless you promise not to tell anybody.

5 If you happen to see Fred, please tell him to get in touch with me.
6 If I were you, I'd / would buy the house now before the price goes up.
7 If I were you, I wouldn't tell her about it.
8 If you really were / were really a policeman, you would have some form of identification.
9 If you paid more attention in class, you wouldn't find the work (so) difficult.
10 If she didn't have flu, she could / would go to the party.
11 If I knew his address, I could / would post it to him.
12 If I were a few years younger, I would apply for that job.
13 If he hadn't been so rude to me, I wouldn't have shouted at him.
14 If the service had been good / better, we would have left a tip.
15 If it hadn't been raining, we would have gone out.
16 If he hadn't been listening to some music, he would have heard them come in.
17 If I had had time, I would have made you a birthday cake.
18 If I had known he was going to be there, I wouldn't have gone.
19 If you had listened to my advice, you wouldn't be in trouble now.
20 If you hadn't drunk so much / If you had drunk less last night, you wouldn't have a splitting headache this morning.

Spotlight on adverbs

1 slowly 2 fast 3 extremely 4 carefully 5 dreadfully 6 well
7 incredibly 8 easily 9 fantastically 10 logically 11 hard 12 angrily
13 heavily 14 late 15 gently

Reading: *High in the sky*

1 a 2 d 3 b 4 d 5 b

Spotlight on vocabulary: work

1 employer 2 application 3 teaching post 4 be dismissed 5 sacked
6 vacant 7 referees 8 qualifications 9 judgement 10 steady
11 redundant 12 extra wages 13 colleagues 14 do 15 fee
16 occupation 17 permit 18 out of work 19 seeking 20 idle

Spotlight on prepositions

1 to, for 2 for 3 of 4 for 5 to 6 of 7 of 8 to 9 for 10 for
11 of 12 for, to 13 to 14 of 15 for

Spotlight on verbs

Thank you again for the lovely time we *had* last weekend. It *was* very kind of you *to invite* us *to stay* with you in the country, and both Theresa and I thoroughly *enjoyed* ourselves. Unfortunately, when we *got* back home we *found* that our house *had been burgled*. We *are* now seriously *thinking* of *moving* to the country, because this *is* the second time we *have been burgled*. In any case, we *have grown / are growing* tired of city life and we both *feel* it *is* time we *made* a firm decision *to leave* London once and for all.
We *would be* grateful if you *could send* us details of any properties for sale near where you *live*. I *'ll / will write* to you soon.

Unit 5

Accuracy building 1

1 a 2 d 3 c 4 c 5 a 6 a 7 b 8 a 9 b 10 c 11 c 12 d
13 a 14 c 15 d 16 b 17 d 18 c 19 b 20 d 21 c 22 b
23 c 24 d 25 c

Accuracy building 2

1 ages 2 believe 3 anxious 4 sentenced 5 hung 6 in 7 out 8 out
9 transmitted 10 doing 11 consists 12 breathe 13 set 14 Bank
15 Let go 16 cake 17 beat 18 permission 19 out 20 laying
21 spotlessly 22 Light 23 lord 24 long 25 corkscrew

Spotlight on expressing preference

1 I prefer the blue jumper to the red one.
2 She prefers swimming to jogging.
3 I'd prefer to leave tonight rather than tomorrow morning.
4 They'd rather go by train than (travel) by coach.
5 She'd prefer not to talk about it.
6 I'd rather you didn't mention this to anyone.
7 We'd rather you didn't visit her just yet.
8 I'd rather he painted the kitchen first.
9 I'd rather the work was done by a professional builder.
10 He'd sooner go to prison than pay the fine.

Spotlight on relative pronouns

1 who 2 whose 3 that / which 4 which 5 which 6 that , who
7 that 8 who 9 who / whom 10 whom 11 that 12 which
13 that / which 14 which 15 which
The relative pronoun can be omitted in statements 3, 7, 9, 11 and 13.

Reading: *Tragedy at sea*

1 b 2 d 3 c 4 b 5 d

Spotlight on vocabulary: water transport

1 voyage 2 liner 3 Channel 4 oars 5 yacht 6 hovercraft 7 sailor
8 steer 9 high tide 10 downstream 11 flow 12 admiral 13 in distress
14 in his cabin 15 at sea 16 waves 17 bank 18 barge 19 when the sea is rough 20 dockers

Spotlight on prepositions

1 on 2 in 3 in 4 for 5 for 6 in 7 of 8 of 9 off 10 of
11 with 12 of 13 with, on 14 of 15 of

Spotlight on verbs

Some months ago three rather absent-minded university professors *arrived* at a station just as the last train of the day *was* about *to leave.* They *ran* to the platform where the train *was* already *moving* slowly out of the station.
'Quick!' *shouted* one of the professors. He *succeeded* in *opening* one of the carriage doors, and two of them *managed to jump* aboard. The third, however, *slipped* and *fell* flat on the platform.
The train *disappeared,* and a porter *hurried* over to the professor who *was lying* on the ground. *Helping / Having helped* the professor to his feet, the porter *asked* him:
'*Have* you *hurt* yourself?'
'No, I *'m / am* fine. I *haven't broken* anything.'
'Well, at least your two friends *caught / have caught* the train,' *said* the porter.
'But I *don't think* they *will be* very happy when they *realise* what they *have done,*' *replied* the professor, *shaking* his head. 'They only *came* to the station *to see* me off.

Key

Unit 6

Accuracy building 1

1 c 2 d 3 a 4 c 5 c 6 d 7 c 8 a 9 d 10 b 11 c 12 d
13 b 14 a 15 b 16 c 17 d 18 b 19 a 20 b 21 d 22 c
23 c 24 b 25 a

Accuracy building 2

1 on 2 expression 3 shrink 4 off 5 have taken 6 meet 7 rises
8 deal 9 feather 10 gate 11 staggering 12 imagine 13 flooded
14 would 15 filthy 16 set 17 off 18 interest 19 speechless 20 broke
21 to 22 stung 23 hopes 24 came 25 rains

Spotlight on liking and disliking

1 He likes to go to the cinema at least twice a month.
2 I found the programme amusing.
3 She didn't think much of the book.
4 I object to his behaviour / the way he behaves.
5 The film depressed her / made her feel depressed.
6 I don't feel like going out tonight.
7 I am definitely not looking forward to my next visit to the dentist's.
8 His visit gave her great / a lot of pleasure.
9 He doesn't approve of such conduct.
10 I can't stand / bear her. She is so arrogant.
11 She doesn't mind baby-sitting now and again.
12 He is dissatisfied with your work.
13 He is disliked by everybody in the class.
14 She is full of admiration for him.
15 The audience applauded loudly / burst into loud applause.

Spotlight on prefixes

1 unable 2 incapable 3 dishonest 4 discourteous 5 impolite
6 unpleasant 7 disagreeable 8 illegible 9 illegal 10 inaccurate
11 disloyal 12 impatient 13 irresponsible 14 inefficient , u nreliable
15 inexperienced 16 unfamiliar 17 unfashionable 18 unfortunate
19 unkind 10 unsatisfactory

Spotlight on prepositions

1 about 2 of 3 of 4 by 5 in 6 under 7 Under 8 for 9 in, on
10 on 11 by 12 for 13 of 14 in 15 of

Reading: *Keep on running*

1 b 2 a 3 d 4 b 5 c

Spotlight on vocabulary: sport

1 pitch 2 spectator 3 foul 4 coach 5 out of practice 6 net 7 bat
8 indoor 9 club_ 10 saddle 11 part 12 by using a whip 13 ring
14 target 15 bow 16 tracksuit 17 oval 18 slope 19 fan
20 disqualified

Spotlight on verbs

Thank you for your letter which I *received* this morning. It *was* lovely *to hear* from you again after so many years. How long *is it* / *has it been* since we last *wrote* to each other? Five

years? Six? Anyway, I *am* so glad that you *have decided to get* in touch with your old friends again.
You *say / said* in your letter that you *are* now married and that you *are expecting* your first child in June. Lucky you! I *am* still *going* out with Roy, *do* you *remember* him? We *have been going* out for more than seven years now, and he still *hasn't / has not asked* me *to marry* him! He *keeps telling* me he *loves* me, but I *am beginning to have* my doubts. What *would* you *do* if you *were* in my position?
Anyway, we *'ll / will / shall have* plenty of time *to talk* about such things next week when you *come* down to London. I *am* really *looking* forward *to seeing* you again and, of course, I *am dying to meet* your husband!
You *ask / asked* in your letter whether Saturday *will / would be* a convenient day for us *to meet*. No problem! Just *give* me a ring as soon as you *arrive* at your hotel.

Unit 7

Accuracy building 1

1 c 2 a 3 b 4 d 5 d 6 a 7 c 8 a 9 d 10 b 11 d 12 b
13 c 14 b 15 c 16 c 17 d 18 c 19 a 20 c 21 b 22 b
23 d 24 c 25 b

Accuracy building 2

1 pain 2 insist 3 swarm 4 allowed 5 Nor do I 6 out 7 you to know
8 running 9 crept 10 achieved 11 cheer up 12 fined 13 fog 14 turn
15 overcome 16 lift 17 monastery 18 erupted 19 cause 20 struck
21 fertile 22 held 23 between 24 looking 25 didn't

Spotlight on certainty, probability and possibility

1 You must be mistaken.
2 He must have been joking.
3 She must have hidden it somewhere in this room.
4 The fire must have been started deliberately.
5 There is no doubt (whatsoever) that she murdered her husband.
6 Is it certain (that) there will not be any buses running tomorrow?
7 I know for certain (that) he will not sign that document.
8 Prices are bound to rise again within the next two months.
9 It's quite likely (that) I'll be late tomorrow.
10 It's likely to rain this afternoon.
11 You are likely to be promoted soon.
12 There are likely to be a lot of people there at that time of day.
13 She can't be your mother! She looks far too young.
14 I couldn't have done it without your help.
15 He can't have been serious.
16 Somebody may have taken it by mistake.
17 Perhaps Mark will lend you the money. Why don't you ask him?
18 Take a map and compass with you in case you get lost.
19 Take a warm coat in case it gets cold tonight.
20 He has a good chance of passing the exam.

Spotlight on *as* and *like*

1 As 2 As 3 like 4 as 5 as 6 as 7 as 8 like 9 as 10 like
11 as 12 as 13 like 14 as 15 as 16 as 17 like

Key

Reading: *Not so perfect*

1 b   2 a   3 d   4 c   5 b

Spotlight on vocabulary: science and technology

1 dissolve   2 expand   3 absorb   4 laboratory   5 microscope   6 carry out
7 synthetic   8 drill   9 petrol   10 atmosphere   11 in orbit   12 launch
13 sound barrier   14 program   15 data   16 lens   17 screen
18 meteorologists   19 ecology   20 current

Spotlight on prepositions

1 for   2 between   3 with   4 with   5 for   6 of   7 of   8 with   9 in
10 on   11 on   12 in   13 of   14 for   15 on

Spotlight on verbs

1 What size (shoes /shirt) do you take?
2 From which platform does the train leave / Which platform does the train leave from?
3 Have you ever been to Scotland?
4 Do you mind if I open a window / Would you mind if I opened a window?
5 (For) how long have you know him / How long have you known him for?
6 Could you describe the man / Could you give me a description of the man?
7 Who broke the window / vase?
8 Have you got / Do you have a receipt?
9 How do I get to / Could you direct me to the town centre?
10 What's your new flat like?
11 Can I take / Would you like to leave a message?
12 What's that called in English?
13 Are you ready to / Would you like to order?
14 Would you like me to give you a hand? / Shall I carry it for you?
15 Would you like / care for a drink / sandwich?

Unit 8

Accuracy building 1

1 b   2 b   3 a   4 c   5 d   6 a   7 d   8 d   9 c   10 c   11 a   12 b
13 b   14 c   15 a   16 c   17 a   18 c   19 d   20 d   21 c   22 a
23 d   24 b   25 a

Accuracy building 2

1 present   2 to you   3 game   4 due   5 up   6 takes   7 by   8 return
9 hopping   10 nap   11 flights   12 mislaying   13 stir   14 make   15 rare
16 sprained   17 sigh   18 is   19 up   20 redundant   21 undoubtedly
22 last   23 mow   24 a day   25 kill

Spotlight on wishing, regretting and apologising

1 I wish Michael could come with us.
2 I wish I could speak French.
3 Betty wishes she didn't have to go to school.
4 I wish I lived in a nicer area.
5 I wish you wouldn't keep / would stop interrupting me!
6 I wish you would stop arguing!
7 I wish I had learned / learnt to play the guitar when I was younger.
8 I wish I hadn't bought the car.

9 They wish to book a room for the night.
10 If only I had some money on me.
11 If only it would stop raining.
12 If only you had told me earlier.
13 I ought to have informed you.
14 I apologise for disturbing you so late at night, but the matter is rather urgent.
15 I think you ought to apologise to her.
16 Andrew apologised to Mary for being / having been so rude to her the night before / the previous evening.
17 You should ask him for an apology.
18 I am sorry to have kept you waiting.
19 We are sorry for any inconvenience that the delay may have caused.
20 The hotel is full, I am afraid.

Spotlight on the definite article

1 – 2 the name the hospital 3 – 4 – 5 the school 6 The doctor 7 the bed 8 the beds 9 – 10 the people /the room 11 The people 12 the piano 13 – 14 – 15 the greatest 16 – 17 the wine 18 the British weather 19 – 20 –

Reading: *Daylight robbery*

1 d 2 a 3 c 4 c 5 c

Spotlight on vocabulary: crime and punishment

1 steal 2 victim 3 robbed of 4 witnessing 5 charged with 6 offence 7 swear to tell the truth 8 verdict 9 sentenced 10 manslaughter 11 bigamy 12 the judge 13 sober 14 break into houses 15 hijack 16 smuggled 17 sue 18 arson 19 abolished 20 barristers

Spotlight on phrasal verbs

1 He broke down and cried like a child.
2 We have decided to break off relations with our neighbouring countries.
3 The police broke up the crowd of angry demonstrators.
4 Our marriage broke up because he drank too much.
5 The fire broke out on the second floor of the building.
6 I was brought up by an aunt in Scotland.
7 What has brought about the sudden change in company policy?
8 Are there any other points you wish to bring up?
9 Throw some water on her face. That should bring her round.
10 It was a difficult deal to negotiate but he managed to bring it off.

Spotlight on completion

1 were 2 so 3 that 4 earn 5 by 6 towards 7 might 8 climbed 9 himself / there 10 in 11 hiding 12 had 13 the / their 14 by 15 sight 16 up / quickly 17 out 18 amazed / astonished / surprised 19 sorts / kinds 20 another

Unit 9

Accuracy building 1

1 b 2 c 3 a 4 c 5 b 6 c 7 a 8 d 9 d 10 c 11 b 12 a 13 d 14 c 15 c 16 b 17 c 18 d 19 b 20 b 21 b 22 a 23 d 24 a 25 d

Key

Accuracy building 2

1 vote 2 head-on 3 issued 4 plot 5 left 6 features 7 behalf
8 enabled 9 account 10 leaking 11 coat 12 admitted 13 consult
14 call 15 ripe 16 heart 17 conducted 18 at 19 shift 20 with
21 advance 22 fell 23 worn 24 audible 25 trumpet

Spotlight on offering, requesting and refusing

1 Would you like me to hoover the carpet for you?
2 She offered Tony a brandy.
3 He offered to do the shopping for his mother.
4 I offered to lend Mr Smith my lawn-mower.
5 He made me an offer of £500 for the furniture.
6 It was such a good offer that he couldn't refuse it / It was too good an offer for him to refuse.
7 I don't suppose you could lend me £700, could you?
8 Would you mind not whistling? I am trying to concentrate.
9 Do you mind if I use your telephone?
10 Would you mind if I took a day off work next week?
11 He begged Carol not to leave him.
12 She refused to let Michael watch / to allow Michael to watch television until he had done his homework.
13 His refusal to co-operate surprised nobody / didn't surprise anybody.
14 Nobody was allowed / permitted to enter the building until it had been thoroughly searched.
15 He refused me permission to quote from his book.

Spotlight on question tags

1 doesn't he 2 hasn't she 3 did you 4 didn't she 5 have you
6 weren't you 7 hadn't you 8 wouldn't she 9 wasn't it 10 can't he
11 aren't there 12 won't you 13 aren't I 14 shall we 15 will / would you

Reading: *Kindness to animals*

1 d 2 c 3 b 4 d 5 c

Spotlight on vocabulary: animals

1 mutton 2 venison 3 veal 4 stable 5 puppies 6 bark 7 howl
8 let the cat out of the bag 9 tame 10 bull 11 trunk 12 geese
13 scarecrow 14 as blind as a bat 15 butterflies 16 duck 17 herd of cattle
18 crawl 19 squirrel 20 migrate

Spotlight on phrasal verbs

1 The football match has been called off.
2 My brother has been called up.
3 The job calls for a certain amount of tact and discretion.
4 He called out to her to attract her attention.
5 The vicar said he would call on them.
6 He has been called away on business. I'm afraid he won't be back until the day after tomorrow.
7 Please carry on with your work.
8 A soldier is punished if he does not carry out an order.
9 I don't think that style of dress will catch on.
10 He is too far ahead. I'll never catch up with him.

Spotlight on completion

1 usual 2 shopping 3 let 4 had 5 On 6 discovered / found 7 had 8 As / Since / Because 9 once 10 used / happened 11 same 12 shaking 13 How 14 without 15 little / bit 16 going 17 for 18 out 19 will 20 forbidden / illegal

Unit 10

Accuracy building 1

1 d 2 c 3 c 4 a 5 b 6 b 7 c 8 a 9 b 10 d 11 d 12 a 13 d 14 c 15 a 16 d 17 d 18 a 19 c 20 a 21 c 22 c 23 b 24 b 25 a

Accuracy building 2

1 held 2 gazed 3 rehearsal 4 park 5 on 6 dare 7 aches 8 ashamed 9 gone 10 bald 11 launched 12 determined 13 either 14 marched 15 through 16 for 17 whispered 18 worthless 19 measured 20 hatch 21 tip 22 had asked 23 as far as 24 with 25 up

Spotlight on conjunctions

1 Although he is rich, he is not happy.
2 Despite his lack of experience / inexperience, I still think he should be promoted.
3 Despite the fact that he is severely handicapped, he is always cheerful and full of life.
4 In spite of his very quick temper, he is a very good manager.
5 He refuses to sell his company even though he made a huge loss last year.
6 Even if they offer me £10 million, I shall still not sell the painting.
7 I'll inform you as soon as I have any news.
8 On arriving home, she discovered that she had left her keys at the office.
9 Just as I was leaving, the postman arrived.
10 I will go as long as you accompany me.
11 Not only does he play the piano, but he also plays three other instruments.
12 I set off early so as to avoid / so that I might avoid any heavy traffic on the roads.
13 It looks as if / though you have made a very big mistake.
14 The airport is closed because there is / because of / due to / owing to / on account of ice on the runways.
15 He was awarded a medal because he had been so / very brave.

Spotlight on *(be/get) used to*

1 She *used to play* tennis at least twice a week when she was younger.
2 You will soon *get used to getting* up early.
3 I *am not used to working* in a restaurant.
4 When I lived in the country, I *used to go* for long walks every day.
5 I *am used to driving* an automatic car.
6 She *used to be* my best friend.
7 There *used to be* a church at the corner, but it was pulled down a few years ago.
8 I *am not used to staying* up late.
9 He never *used to be* so mean.
10 He *isn't used to living* on his own.

Reading: *Appropriate dress*

1 c 2 a 3 c 4 d 5 c

Key

Spotlight on vocabulary: dress

1 cloth 2 woven 3 a needle and thread 4 untie 5 match 6 gloves
7 under 8 inside 9 overalls 10 belt 11 very loose 12 shabby
13 beggar 14 wrist 15 necklace 16 take it up 17 try on
18 you have got your clothes on 19 undo 20 wrap yourself up well

Spotlight on phrasal verbs

1 She came round a few minutes ago.
2 She has come into a fortune.
3 A problem has come up regarding the new contract.
4 We didn't expect to come up against such a problem.
5 The new magazine is coming out tomorrow.
6 I came across it as I was clearing out the attic.
7 Nobody has come up with a solution to the problem.
8 Come on or we'll be late.
9 During a sale, prices come down.
10 Why don't you come round (to our house) one evening next week?

Spotlight on completion

1 cities / towns 2 whose 3 it 4 for 5 only 6 would 7 what
8 him 9 who / that 10 enough 11 own 12 how 13 waste 14 down
15 spent 16 persuade / get 17 notice 18 make 19 in 20 by

Unit 11

Accuracy building 1

1 b 2 c 3 c 4 b 5 b 6 d 7 a 8 d 9 b 10 d 11 a 12 b
13 d 14 d 15 c 16 d 17 c 18 d 19 b 20 b 21 d 22 a
23 d 24 c 25 c

Accuracy building 2

1 in 2 to 3 pat 4 iceberg 5 view 6 draught 7 envy 8 direct
9 clap 10 tales 11 to 12 you did it 13 fallen 14 Overhearing
15 trunks 16 peckish 17 proverb 18 peel 19 mood 20 gasped
21 looks up to 22 wrinkled 23 poke 24 said 25 terms

Spotlight on the gerund or infinitive (1)

1 I remember seeing that film two years ago.
2 He remembered to send her a birthday card.
3 I don't remember mentioning it to anyone.
4 Someone tried to kill / assassinate / murder the President.
5 Try pressing the red button.
6 She tried to smile even though she was in great pain.
7 Try adjusting the aerial.
8 Please stop making so much noise.
9 He stopped to check the brakes.
10 They stop serving lunch at three o'clock.
11 It was very nice of you to write to me.
12 It was wrong of you to criticise her in front of the others.
13 It wasn't necessary (for you) to go to so much trouble.
14 I didn't mean to do it.
15 If I accept the job, it will mean losing my place at university.

16 I will earn more money in my new job, but it will mean working / having to work longer hours.
17 Tony helped me (to) decorate my flat.
18 He couldn't help laughing.
19 The tablets helped me (to) get over my depression.
20 I can't help feeling sorry for her.

Reading: *Stranger than fiction*

1 b 2 c 3 c 4 d 5 a

Spotlight on adjectives ending in *-ing* or *-ed*

1 exhausted 2 amusing 3 disappointing 4 interesting 5 shocked
6 thrilling 7 puzzled 8 worried 9 annoying 10 terrifying
11 disgusting 12 pleased 13 exciting 14 fascinating 15 bored
16 surprised 17 confusing 18 impressed 19 embarrassing 20 tiring

Spotlight on vocabulary: fact and fiction

1 mirage 2 frightened 3 imaginative 4 vivid 5 made up 6 truthful
7 state 8 a work of fiction 9 dream 10 tricks 11 taken in 12 misleading
13 difficult to believe 14 character in a book 15 a realist 16 day-dreamer
17 incredible 18 beyond belief 19 eyes 20 unidentified flying object

Spotlight on phrasal verbs

1 Why did you cut it up?
2 He was advised to cut down on the amount of meat he ate.
3 The water rose higher and higher and I suddenly found myself cut off from the rest of the group.
4 The van drew up outside the cinema and two men jumped out.
5 I'll draw out some money from the bank this afternoon.
6 Make sure that the contract is drawn up by a good lawyer.
7 The kitchen walls could do with a fresh coat of paint.
8 When did you do up the kitchen? It looks really smart.
9 They ought to do away with such an absurd law.
10 We must do without a holiday this year.

Spotlight on completion

1 set 2 for 3 None 4 what 5 was 6 no 7 nobody / no-one 8 on
9 searched 10 without 11 Something 12 in 13 looked 14 hung
15 plenty 16 its 17 had 18 have 19 there 20 such

Unit 12

Accuracy building 1

1 c 2 c 3 d 4 b 5 a 6 a 7 d 8 c 9 b 10 b 11 a 12 d
13 d 14 c 15 a 16 d 17 d 18 c 19 d 20 c 21 a 22 a
23 d 24 b 25 b

Accuracy building 2

1 distorted 2 receive 3 make 4 spilt 5 fierce 6 might 7 blinds
8 for 9 ambition 10 accompany 11 in the middle of 12 tell 13 shelter
14 packed 15 lying 16 hand 17 snack 18 glimpse 19 spoil
20 overcast 21 leap 22 chilly 23 tide 24 on 25 see

Key

Spotlight on the gerund or nfinitive (2)

1 It is a criminal offence to drive while under the influence of alcohol.
2 It's very bad manners to speak with your mouth full.
3 I saw him shoot his wife.
4 He heard somebody coming up the stairs, so he switched off the light and hid under the bed.
5 I saw her take some money from the till.
6 She regretted slapping him across the face.
7 She denied stealing the necklace.
8 He refused to hand over the document.
9 He failed to keep his promise.
10 He threatened to kill me if I didn't follow his instructions.
11 He warned me not to touch the wire.
12 I hate to trouble you at this time of night, but I think you ought to know what has happened.
13 I hate getting up early on a cold wintry morning.
14 In my opinion, the film is not worth seeing.
15 There's no point (in) discussing the matter with him.
16 Nothing is going to prevent me from doing my duty.
17 To avoid upsetting her, he didn't mention what had happened.
18 You risk losing everything.
19 Have you ever considered working abroad?
20 How about going out for a drink?
21 I was on the point of saying something when I noticed my boss at the other end of the room.
22 I can't imagine living anywhere else. I'm very happy where I am now.
23 What caused him to react so violently?
24 I didn't choose to leave my country.
25 I've finished painting the room.

Reading: *Passport to eternity*

1 d 2 c 3 c 4 b 5 a

Spotlight on vocabulary: health

1 send for 2 break out 3 got over 4 go down with 5 bleed 6 heal
7 on a stretcher 8 in plaster 9 sore 10 blisters 11 surgery
12 prescriptions 13 do 14 unwell 15 cough 16 severe 17 passed out
18 an optician 19 first aid kit 20 cotton wool

Spotlight on word formation: nouns

1 generosity 2 curiosity 3 anxiety 4 inventor 5 instructor
6 instructions 7 waitress 8 attendant 9 employment 10 employees
11 applicant 12 application 13 identification 14 admission 15 advice
16 practice 17 length 18 shortage 19 depth 20 strength 21 weight
22 height 23 width 24 beauty 25 wealth

Spotlight on phrasal verbs

1 Do you have any savings you can fall back on?
2 Demand for their products has fallen off this year.
3 I fell for her the moment I saw her.
4 He fell out with his best friend.
5 My plans have fallen through.
6 How is he getting on in his new job?

7 The thieves got away in a stolen car.
8 She has to get by on £40 a week.
9 When will you get round to mending the fuse?
10 Don't let it get you down.
11 He is getting on for sixty.
12 I phoned several times, but I couldn't get through to him.

Spotlight on completion

1 There 2 at 3 such 4 had 5 body / corpse 6 become / been
7 carried 8 playing 9 result / consequence 10 occasion 11 many
12 made 13 which 14 would 15 highly / very / most 16 pulled 17 all
18 to 19 then / afterwards 20 of

Unit 13

Accuracy building 1

1 b 2 c 3 c 4 d 5 c 6 b 7 a 8 a 9 c 10 b 11 c 12 a
13 c 14 a 15 d 16 a 17 b 18 a 19 d 20 b 21 d 22 d
23 b 24 a 25 c

Accuracy building 2

1 overlooks 2 went 3 awarded 4 up for 5 message 6 about
7 to meeting 8 sleepy 9 scolded 10 poured 11 hands 12 let
13 shattered 14 robbed 15 whatever 16 roared 17 tail 18 standstill
19 sensible 20 hitched 21 strap 22 into 23 soaked 24 cover
25 extinct

Spotlight on time constructions (1)

1 Michael has been collecting stamps for ten years (now).
2 I've had this watch since my fifteenth birthday / I was fifteen / the age of fifteen.
3 She has been playing the violin since she was eight / the age of eight.
4 When did you start / begin smoking / to smoke?
5 He hasn't eaten meat for five years (now).
6 I learned to drive when I was eighteen.
7 It's ten years since I (last) went to the theatre.
8 It's ages since I (last) saw a good film.
9 It's over thirty years since I (first) started / began working for this company.
10 The last time I saw her was ten years ago.
11 The last time you wrote to me was in January.
12 How long is it since they moved to Scotland?
13 How long is it since you last went to the dentist's?
14 I first met her / I met her for the first time at a fancy-dress party.
15 It's the first time he has been late.
16 It's the first time I have seen him in such a foul mood.
17 I plan to spend three months in France.
18 We spent the whole day lying on the beach.
19 It took me two hours to write that composition.
20 He cycled to work in twenty minutes.

Spotlight on word formation: nouns

1 carelessness 2 failure 3 privacy 4 poverty 5 shyness 6 photography
7 photographer 8 winner 9 loss 10 loan 11 responsibility
12 competition 13 competitors 14 dependants 15 pronunciation

16 assistance 17 comparison 18 recovery 19 explanation 20 Necessity
21 choice 22 complaint 23 heat 24 threat 25 extent

Reading: *Queen of romance*

1 b 2 c 3 b 4 c 5 d

Spotlight on vocabulary: relationships

1 bring up 2 related 3 a relation of yours 4 niece 5 stepfather
6 brother-in-law 7 widower 8 bachelor 9 her hand in marriage 10 reject
11 feelings 12 about 13 bride 14 reception 15 apart 16 lost interest
17 give 18 pen pal 19 the cold shoulder 20 crazy about

Spotlight on phrasal verbs

1 The milk has gone off.
2 I've decided to go in for that particular competition.
3 The fire alarm went off and we all left the building.
4 Those trousers don't go with your jacket.
5 The fire went out.
6 Please go on. I'm listening.
7 I went after the thief but he escaped.
8 He went back on his promise.
9 Time goes by quickly when you are enjoying yourself.
10 The bomb went off and killed three people.
11 We need to go through / over the accounts.
12 I hope there will be enough food to go round.
13 Make sure you go over these phrasal verbs.
14 The dog went for the postman.

Spotlight on completion

1 whom 2 took 3 which / that 4 so 5 every 6 what 7 was 8 as
9 that 10 told 11 by 12 even 13 of 14 have 15 realised 16 at
17 help 18 how 19 in 20 until

Unit 14

Accuracy building 1

1 d 2 a 3 d 4 b 5 b 6 a 7 d 8 d 9 c 10 a 11 c
12 b 13 c 14 b 15 b 16 c 17 a 18 b 19 c 20 b 21 a
22 b 23 c 24 b 25 c

Accuracy building 2

1 of 2 consent 3 Should 4 regardless 5 express 6 fail 7 rank
8 review 9 to 10 in 11 straight 12 shadow 13 regular 14 way
15 times 16 take 17 restore 18 anchor 19 settle 20 delinquents
21 shaking 22 did 23 sip 24 broad 25 guessed

Spotlight on time constructions (2)

1 By the time he retires, he will have written twenty novels.
2 By this time next year, I shall / will have been working / have worked for the same company for thirty years.
3 By next April I will have been in England for one year.
4 I have been teaching English at Felton College for twenty-seven years.
5 By the time the firemen arrived, the children had (already) put out the fire.

6 By the time he was twenty, he had become the company's top sales person.
7 By the time I received her letter, she had (already) left for Italy.
8 I didn't realise until later what a terrible mistake I had made.
9 It wasn't until I opened my handbag that I discovered my credit cards had been stolen.
10 No sooner had they arrived home than they started quarrelling.
11 Never have I been so insulted in all my life!
12 It's time for us to leave.
13 It's time you were in bed.
14 It's about time you decided what to do.
15 It's high time he was taught a lesson.
16 The roof hasn't been repaired yet.
17 He can't see you right now because he is busy showing a client around the factory.
18 After visiting Tom, we called in to see Ann.
19 Before going home, we did some shopping in Oxford street.
20 The report must be completed by Friday.

Spotlight on word formation: adjectives

1 trusting / trustful 2 trustworthy 3 reliable 4 sensitive 5 worthless
6 worthy 7 dependent 8 dependable 9 classic 10 classical 11 frightful
12 economic 13 economical 14 educational 15 frozen 16 childish
17 restless 18 helpless 19 hopeless 20 pitiful 21 unforgettable
22 forgetful 23 plentiful 24 delightful 25 priceless

Reading: *Public entertainment*

1 d 2 b 3 b 4 a 5 d

Spotlight on vocabulary: entertainment

1 audience 2 usherette 3 rows 4 rehearse 5 dress 6 screen
7 scenery 8 put on 9 lines 10 interval 11 clapping 12 director
13 shoot 14 adjust 15 channels 16 disc jockey 17 flash 18 bouncers
19 studio 20 success

Spotlight on phrasal verbs

1 I forgot to hand in my homework.
2 Have you handed out all the leaflets?
3 Hand over the money or I'll shoot you!
4 He stamped my passport and then handed it back to me.
5 Please don't hang up! What I have to say is very important.
6 There is a suspicious-looking man hanging about / around near the entrance.
7 We were held up by the traffic.
8 Could you hold on, please? I'll try and put you through.
9 Three banks have been held up in the past two days.
10 He has never been able to hold down a job for more than a couple of months.

Spotlight on completion

1 at / on 2 get 3 on 4 side 5 hat 6 in 7 which 8 ground / pavement 9 From 10 before 11 clothes 12 off 13 beside 14 looked
15 what 16 until 17 hour 18 stopped 19 To 20 could

Key

Unit 15

Accuracy building 1

1 a   2 b   3 c   4 b   5 c   6 d   7 d   8 a   9 c   10 d   11 b
12 b   13 d   14 b   15 c   16 a   17 a   18 c   19 b   20 a   21 b
22 c   23 a   24 b   25 c

Accuracy building 2

1 struck   2 up   3 run   4 belongings   5 stale   6 dressed   7 meet
8 giving off   9 label   10 into   11 saying   12 greenhouse   13 coffin
14 off   15 down   16 than   17 arranged   18 antiseptic   19 torch
20 fiddle   21 appliance   22 for   23 earth   24 pinch   25 chatterbox

Spotlight on *too, enough, so* and *such*

1 There is too much sugar in this tea.
2 There is not enough petrol in the tank.
3 She's not old enough to go out on her own.
4 You didn't try hard enough.
5 I don't have enough money to buy you a decent present.
6 It was too dark for us to see where we were going.
7 It's too difficult a book for children to read.
8 I was so frightened (that) I couldn't / didn't say anything.
9 The coffee was too hot (for me) to drink.
10 She is such a spoilt child that nobody likes her.
11 We had such bad luck yesterday.
12 I didn't realise it would be such hard work.
13 It was such a hot day that we decided to go for a swim in the lake.
14 I've got such a lot of things to do this morning.
15 So rarely do I see this student that I've forgotten his name.

Spotlight on word formation: verbs

1 overcharged   2 disqualified   3 misbehaving   4 overtake   5 mistook
6 mislead   7 misunderstood   8 identify   9 criticising   10 enlarged
11 overcome   12 strengthening   13 soften   14 shorten   15 widened
16 deepened   17 discourage   18 encourage   19 misplaced   20 overcooked
21 deafened   22 saddened   23 tightening   24 loosened   25 broadens

Reading: *Waiting to pay*

1 d   2 d   3 a   4 c   5 b

Spotlight on vocabulary: eating and drinking

1 napkin   2 crockery   3 saucepan   4 bowl   5 slice   6 chopped
7 potatoes   8 beaten   9 jam   10 tasty   11 swallowed   12 roll
13 teaspoon   14 spread   15 in the oven   16 raw   17 pint   18 dry
19 starving   20 hangover

Spotlight on phrasal verbs

1 Everybody looks up to him.
2 She looks down on her neighbours.
3 I shall look into the matter.
4 They just looked on.
5 Look out! There's a car coming towards you.
6 He looked up and smiled.
7 He looked up her number in the telephone directory.

8 She will look after you when I am gone.
9 After looking round the house, we decided not to buy it.
10 When revising, you should look over / through all the exercises in this book.
11 He grabbed my handbag and made for the door.
12 I could just make out the road sign through the fog.
13 The thieves made off with the jewels.
14 Did you make up that story?
15 Nothing could make up for the loss of his parents.

Spotlight on completion

1 at 2 in 3 left 4 where 5 previous / last 6 due / going 7 an
8 would / might 9 time 10 after 11 reserved 12 would 13 There
14 that 15 took 16 expected 17 to 18 finding 19 reached
20 departure

Unit 16

Accuracy building 1

1 c 2 d 3 b 4 d 5 d 6 a 7 b 8 d 9 c 10 b 11 b
12 d 13 a 14 c 15 c 16 c 17 c 18 a 19 c 20 d 21 a
22 c 23 c 24 a 25 c

Accuracy building 2

1 loaded 2 sharp 3 subject 4 report 5 to 6 sobbing 7 built-up
8 cracked 9 memories 10 for 11 orchard 12 as 13 hills 14 What
15 down 16 skin 17 sentence 18 before 19 loaves 20 random
21 stricken 22 in 23 dozed 24 spray 25 consume

Spotlight on description

1 She has shoulder-length hair.
2 He is broad-shouldered.
3 He is middle-aged.
4 She is in her late thirties.
5 I have a ten-year-old daughter.
6 She is broken-hearted.
7 He is of medium height.
8 She is of average intelligence.
9 He is a fairly tall man.
10 Her face is sun-tanned.
11 He was wearing an old brown woollen sweater.
12 She has long blonde wavy hair.
13 She has large round blue eyes.
14 It was an eight-hour flight.
15 It is a three-month course.
16 It was a two-day journey.
17 There's a suspicious-looking man near the door.
18 He had sad-looking eyes.
19 He was smartly-dressed for the occasion.
20 He is a badly-behaved child.

Spotlight on *say* and *tell*

1 say 2 told 3 said 4 say 5 said 6 telling 7 told 8 said 9 Tell
10 said 11 tell 12 tell 13 saying 14 tell 15 tell

Reading: *Motorway madness*

1 b 2 a 3 d 4 d 5 a

Spotlight on vocabulary: motoring

1 run out of 2 get into 3 dented 4 skid 5 room 6 swerve 7 bypass
8 diversion 9 flat 10 in 11 licence 12 boot 13 attendant 14 head
15 gear 16 lanes 17 heavy 18 park 19 collided with 20 instructor

Spotlight on phrasal verbs

1 He has put on weight.
2 Can you put me up for the night?
3 The concert has been put off until next week.
4 They put out the fire.
5 She won't put up with bad manners.
6 The old dog was in such pain that there was no alternative but to have it put down.
7 The awful smell from the kitchen put me off my food.
8 They have put up their prices for the third time this year.
9 I am putting some money aside for a rainy day.
10 He put on a French accent.
11 They ran after the thief.
12 He looks worn out.
13 I ran into Jane in the High Street this morning.
14 The team from Halifax ran away with the competition.
15 Eight children have run away from that orphanage in the past year.

Spotlight on completion

1 would 2 at 3 how 4 sentenced 5 on 6 let 7 as 8 ways
9 allowed / permitted 10 after 11 at 12 hit / struck 13 like 14 in
15 of 16 kept 17 just / only / merely 18 have 19 with 20 sent

Unit 17

Accuracy building 1

1 c 2 b 3 a 4 d 5 b 6 d 7 b 8 c 9 b 10 a 11 c 12 d
13 a 14 a 15 c 16 b 17 d 18 c 19 b 20 c 21 b 22 c
23 a 24 b 25 d

Accuracy building 2

1 pulled 2 aroused 3 dusk 4 confirm 5 through 6 on 7 wink
8 broke 9 for 10 blushed 11 set 12 mat 13 drive 14 shortly
15 find 16 drill 17 numb 18 sunk 19 desired 20 for 21 slapped
22 beak 23 crawled 24 late 25 died

Spotlight on some useful grammar points

1 The cottage they live in / where they live / in which they live is at the top of a steep hill.
2 The restaurant she works in / where she works / in which she works is opposite the police station.
3 There's no need to shout.
4 How much did you pay for the car?
5 What was the cause of the fire?
6 What do you do for a living?
7 Who does this camera belong to?

8 Mark borrowed fifty pounds from Andrew last week / Mark owes Andrew fifty pounds.
9 The man (who) I was introduced to / to whom I was introduced had / has friends in high places.
10 There isn't anything left to eat.
11 There's no milk in the fridge.
12 He spoke to me in a friendly manner / way.
13 I found it difficult to concentrate.
14 I haven't received a reply to the letter I wrote to her.
15 On the whole, I am pleased with the progress he is making.

Reading: *Heavy weather*

1 b 2 a 3 b 4 d 5 a

Spotlight on vocabulary: the weather

1 in 2 shower 3 pouring down 4 waterproof 5 cats and dogs
6 rainy 7 droughts 8 chilly 9 severe 10 breeze 11 turn
12 under the weather 13 set in 14 spell 15 mist 16 hail
17 forecast 18 frost 19 lightning 20 storm in a teacup

Spotlight on singular and plural

1 was 2 was 3 is 4 are 5 has 6 is 7 don't 8 these 9 is 10 was
11 are 12 brothers 13 has 14 is 15 dozen 16 another 17 fruit 18 is
19 hundred 20 means

Spotlight on phrasal verbs

1 I didn't take to him at first, but now we are the best of friends.
2 We take on extra staff during the summer season.
3 Why don't you take up a hobby or a sport?
4 I was taken in by his smart appearance and gentle voice. I didn't find out until later that he was a criminal.
5 Our firm has been taken over by a larger company.
6 He takes after his father.
7 Anything you say will be taken down and may be used against you in court.
8 I'm tired. I think I'll turn in.
9 We've decided to turn down their offer.
10 The restaurant was full, so we were turned away.
11 He turned up just as we were about to leave.
12 How did the party turn out? Was it a success?

Spotlight on completion

1 sunset 2 on 3 could 4 in 5 looked 6 At 7 enough 8 after
9 poured 10 ill 11 no 12 so / therefore 13 will / shall 14 with
15 before 16 next 17 along / down / up 18 shone 19 called 20 was